Consent to Being

VERITAS

Series Introduction

"... the truth will set you free" (John 8:32)

In much contemporary discourse, Pilate's question has been taken to mark the absolute boundary of human thought. Beyond this boundary, it is often suggested, is an intellectual hinterland into which we must not venture. This terrain is an agnosticism of thought: because truth cannot be possessed, it must not be spoken. Thus, it is argued that the defenders of "truth" in our day are often traffickers in ideology, merchants of counterfeits, or anti-liberal. They are, because it is somewhat taken for granted that Nietzsche's word is final: truth is the domain of tyranny.

Is this indeed the case, or might another vision of truth offer itself? The ancient Greeks named the love of wisdom as *philia*, or friendship. The one who would become wise, they argued, would be a "friend of truth." For both philosophy and theology might be conceived as schools in the friendship of truth, as a kind of relation. For like friendship, truth is as much discovered as it is made. If truth is then so elusive, if its domain is *terra incognita*, perhaps this is because it arrives to us—unannounced—as gift, as a person, and not some thing.

The aim of the Veritas book series is to publish incisive and original current scholarly work that inhabits "the between" and "the beyond" of theology and philosophy. These volumes will all share a common aspiration to transcend the institutional divorce in which these two disciplines often find themselves, and to engage questions of pressing concern to both philosophers and theologians in such a way as to reinvigorate both disciplines with a kind of interdisciplinary desire, often so absent in contemporary academe. In a word, these volumes represent collective efforts in the befriending of truth, doing so beyond the simulacra of pretend tolerance, the violent, yet insipid reasoning of liberalism that asks with Pilate, "What is truth?"—expecting a consensus of non-commitment; one that encourages the commodification of the mind, now sedated by the civil service of career, ministered by the frightened patrons of position.

The series will therefore consist of two wings: (1) original monographs; and (2) essay collections on a range of topics in theology and philosophy. The latter will principally be the products of the annual conferences of the Centre of Theology and Philosophy (www.theologyphilosophycentre.co.uk).

Conor Cunningham and Joseph Terry, *Veritas Series Editors*

Available from Cascade Books

Anthony D. Baker	*Diagonal Advance: Perfection in Christian Theology*
D. C. Schindler	*The Perfection of Freedom: Schiller, Schelling, and Hegel between the Ancients and the Moderns*
Rustin Brian	*Covering Up Luther: How Barth's Christology Challenged the* Deus Absconditus *that Haunts Modernity*
Timothy Stanley	*Protestant Metaphysics After Karl Barth and Martin Heidegger*
Christopher Ben Simpson	*The Truth Is the Way: Kierkegaard's* Theologia Viatorum
Richard H. Bell	*Wagner's Parsifal: An Appreciation in the Light of His Theological Journey*
Antonio Lopez	*Gift and the Unity of Being*
Toyohiko Kagawa	*Cosmic Purpose*, translated and introduced by Thomas John Hastings
Nigel Zimmerman	*Facing the Other: John Paul II, Levinas, and the Body*
Conor Sweeney	*Sacramental Presence after Heidegger: Onto-theology, Sacraments, and the Mother's Smile*
John Behr et al. (eds.)	*The Role of Death in Life: A Multidisciplinary Examination of the Relation between Life and Death*
Eric Austin Lee et al. (eds.)	*The Resounding Soul: Reflection on the Metaphysics and Vivacity of the Human Person*
Orion Edgar	*Things Seen and Unseen: The Logic of Incarnation in Merleau-Ponty's Metaphysics of Flesh*
Duncan B. Reyburn	*Seeing Things as They Are: G. K. Chesterton and the Drama of Meaning*
Lyndon Shakespeare	*Being the Body of Christ in the Age of Management*
Michael V. Di Fuccia	*Owen Barfield: Philosophy, Poetry, and Theology*
John McNerney	*Wealth of Persons: Economics with a Human Face*
Norm Klassen	*The Fellowship of the Beatific Vision: Chaucer on Overcoming Tyranny and Becoming Ourselves*
Donald Wallenfang	*Human and Divine Being: A Study of the Theological Anthropology of Edith Stein*
Sotiris Mitralexis	*Ever-Moving Repose: A Contemporary Reading of Maximus the Confessor's Theory of Time*
Sotiris Mitralexis et al. (eds.)	*Maximus the Confessor as a European Philosopher*
Kevin Corrigan	*Love, Friendship, Beauty, and the Good: Plato, Aristotle, and the Later Tradition*
Andrew Brower Latz	*The Social Philosophy of Gillian Rose*

1. Note: Nathan Kerr, *Christ, History, and Apocalyptic*, although volume 3 of the original SCM Veritas series, is available from Cascade as part of the Theopolitical Visions series.

D. C. Schindler	*Love and the Postmodern Predicament: Rediscovering the Real in Beauty, Goodness, and Truth*
Stephen Kampowski	*Embracing Our Finitude: Exercises in a Christian Anthropology between Dependence and Gratitude*
William Desmond	*The Gift of Beauty and the Passion of Being: On the Threshold between the Aesthetic and the Religious*
Charles Péguy	*Notes on Bergson and Descartes*
David Alcalde	*Cosmology without God: The Problematic Theology Inherent in Modern Cosmology*
Benson P. Fraser	*Hide and Seek: The Sacred Art of Indirect Communication*
Philip John Paul Gonzales	*Exorcising Philosophical Modernity: Cyril O'Regan and Christian Discourse after Modernity*
Caitlin Smith Gilson	*Subordinated Ethics: Natural Law and Moral Miscellany in Aquinas and Dostoyevsky*
Michael Dominic Taylor	*The Foundations of Nature: Metaphysics of Gift for an Integral Ecological Ethic*
David W. Opderbeck	*The End of the Law? Law, Theology, and Neuroscience*
Caitlin Smith Gilson	*As It Is in Heaven: Some Christian Questions on the Nature of Paradise*
Andrew T. J. Kaethler	*The Eschatological Person: Alexander Schemann and Joseph Ratzinger in Dialogue*
Emmanuel Falque	*By Way of Obstacles: A Pathway through a Work*
Paul Tyson (ed.)	*Astonishment in Science: Engagements with William Desmond*
Darren Dyk	*Will & Love: Shakespeare and the Motion of the Soul*
Matthew Vest	*Ethics Lost in Modernity: Reflections on Wittgenstein and Bioethics*
Hanna Lucas	*Sensing the Sacred: Recovering a Mystagogical Vision of Knowledge and Salvation*
Philip Gonzales et al. (eds.)	*Finitude's Wounded Praise: Responses to Jean-Louis Crétien*
Martin Koci et al. (eds.)	*God and Phenomenology: Thinking with Jean-Yves Lacoste*
Steven E. Knepper (ed.)	*A Heart of Flesh: William Desmond and the Bible*
James Madden	*Thinking About Thinking: Mind and Meaning in the Era of Techno-Nihilism*
Tyler Dalton McNabb	*An Analytic Theology of Evangelism: A Classical Theist's Approach*
Duncan Reyburn	*The Roots of the World: The Remarkable Prescience of G. K. Chesterton*
Pablo Irizar et al. (eds.)	*To Die of Not Writing: Doing Philosophy of Religion with Emmanuel Falque*
Rachel M. Coleman	*Matter as an Image of the Good: Ferdinand Ulrich's Metaphysics of Creation*
Christine Stephenson	*Remembering Augustine: The Symphonic Forms and Fundamental Affordances of Memory in His Theology of Memoria*

Consent to Being

AIMÉ FOREST

Translation and Introduction by Bruce K. Ward

Foreword by John Milbank

CASCADE *Books* • Eugene, Oregon

CONSENT TO BEING

Cascade Books
An Imprint of Wipf and Stock Publishers
199 W. 8th Ave., Suite 3
Eugene, OR 97401

www.wipfandstock.com

PAPERBACK ISBN: 979-8-3852-3972-6
HARDCOVER ISBN: 979-8-3852-3973-3
EBOOK ISBN: 979-8-3852-3974-0

Cataloguing-in-Publication data:

Names: Forest, Aimé [author]. | Ward, Bruce K. [translator]. | Milbank, John [foreword writer].

Title: Consent to being / by Aimé Forest; translated and introduced by Bruce K. Ward ; foreword by John Milbank

Description: Eugene, OR: Cascade Books, 2026 | Series: Veritas | Includes bibliographical references.

Identifiers: ISBN 979-8-3852-3972-6 (paperback) | ISBN 979-8-3852-3973-3 (hardcover) | ISBN 979-8-3852-3974-0 (ebook)

Subjects: LCSH: Forest, Aimé. | Metaphysics. | Spiritualism (Philosophy)—History—20th century. | Ontology. | Idealism.

Classification: B2430.F694 F66 2026 (paperback) | B2430.F694 (ebook)

02/13/26

Originally published in French as *Du consentement à l'être et autres textes.* Paris: Hermann, 2022. Translated with permission.

For Nancy

Contents

Foreword

Aimé Forest in the Twenty-First Century

THE MORE THAT THE millennium year recedes from our view, the more we realize that we no longer live in the twentieth century. One aspect of this realization is to start to wonder just how significant, intellectually and culturally, that century really was. It can now seem as if it was mostly an often literal fighting out of philosophies and ideologies rooted in the previous one, the nineteenth.

Of course, at the outset of the twentieth century, there was a widespread sense of a stark rupture with an epoch now conceived as stuffily tradition-bound. There ensued a converse venturing upon experimentation of a historically unprecedented kind, either in the name of a pure "modern" recommencement, or of a new astringent formalism, but in either case with a certain rejection of historicism and the priority of time.

Yet the fact that this rupture occurred at the very outset of a new century should give us pause. There just had not been time for such drastic changes to have emerged overnight, and whether we are talking about science or the arts of every kind, in fact the early twentieth century took existing new approaches or experiments to admittedly radical new extremes. In physics the traditional Newtonian understanding of matter and of fixed laws had long been challenged, just as in the arts shifts from traditional given forms—from a dominance of the mimetic and from superfluous detail, besides a radical openness at once to the arcane and the demotic—had been under way ever since early Romanticism.

But what is more, it appears to us now in retrospect that the twentieth-century "modern" was not just a bringing of the Victorian to an unexpectedly shocking acme, but also that a double Victorian legacy of both Romanticism and post-Romantic challenges to it—variously positivist, ironic, realist, cynical, fideist, and materialist—persisted.

The anti-Romantic realism of the novel mutated into the more subjective realism of stream of consciousness, but at the same time, and at a more popular level, the long-winded realism of the serial novel was displaced by the shorter fantasy of the adventure story and much genre fiction. In poetry the relationship even of an arch classicist like Ezra Pound to the legacy of the romance and Romanticism remained ambivalent, while soon enough modernist-romantic hybrids appeared in the work of D. H. Lawrence, Dylan Thomas, and Basil Bunting.

Although architectural modernism triumphed, it was for long challenged by the Arts and Crafts and *art nouveau* or *jugendstil* legacies with their greater historical resonance and linkage of conscious formalism to affective memory. In science itself, the covert neo-Newtonianism of Einstein's attempted "total cosmology" was soon challenged by quantum physics with its inherently more "Romantic" commitment to temporal irreversibility and relativity of perspective, that seemed to extend even to the mental and so spiritual. Of course, that tension is still with us today.

As to philosophy, again we are now becoming more aware of the survival of Romantic and nineteenth-century currents into the twentieth. Early analytic philosophy, prior to Frege's Germanic influence, sustained metaphysical concerns, but slightly mutated from "idealism" to "realism." And only R. G. Collingwood's very premature death prevented a survival of "British idealism" from later encountering mutations of both phenomenology and linguistic philosophy that were re-invoking nineteenth-century concerns with the body, with the aesthetic, and with history, in ways with which he might have resonated.

In theology we have to face the shocking fact that the theologically "amateur" work of the Oxford "Inklings" has stood the course of time with the public and even intellectuals much better than the legacy of Barth and Bonhoeffer, which was supposed to mark a rigorous modern break with Romantic subjectivity and its supposedly deficient sense of both tragedy and divine otherness. Yet it is clear that the Inklings were themselves close to the persistence of Oxford idealism in the shape of the "Magdalen Metaphysicals." There is, after all, a philosophical kinship between the Inklings' most key thinker, Owen Barfield, and Collingwood, who conversely was much interested in myth, folk-story, and the "magic" or "enchantment" of art.

The Inklings sustained an essentially Romantic concern with the integration of grace and nature (reinforced by the influence of that Scottish Victorian devotee of Novalis, George Macdonald) through both reason and the imagination. In this respect they were close to the more academic theology of the *nouvelle théologie*, its German equivalent, and to Russian Sophiology. Yet unfortunately the arbitrariness of the typical twentieth-century theology syllabus gave students the impression that Schleiermacher is the crucial representative of theological Romanticism, which is inherently linked with "liberalism." Of course, Schleiermacher is interesting and important (and himself much misunderstood), and yet the over-focus upon him has tended to preclude the significance of the more conservative Romantic legacies of Coleridge, Novalis, the Schlegels, and Schelling, and the very many whom they influenced.

But there is a stronger point to be made than all the foregoing. It is simply arbitrary to assume that the persisting Romantic currents were more conservative and less modern than the modernist ones. I have already indicated how, in the case of physics, the quantum perspective arguably more sustains a nineteenth-century priority for time and perspective. And when it comes to literature, we can see that even the key modernist works themselves are often indebted to Bergson (Proust, Thomas Mann, Woolf) and to Bradley (Eliot, Yeats, Auden—right down to Geoffrey Hill) rather than to the promoters of analysis or phenomenology. Even James Joyce played upon themes in Newman and in Vico. The more austere modernist favoring of space over time by Wyndham Lewis did not really find favor, just as Le Corbusier's formalism was linked to a reactionary neo-Thomism pointing in authoritarian directions, which proved a political dead end, in contrast to Gaudi's democratic Catholic and locally rooted organicism.

When we consider philosophy, then, it is startling to read in his *Autobiography* that Collingwood thinks of "the school of T. H. Green" as the real heirs of Bacon, Locke, Hume, Berkeley, and Coleridge, despite their German influences, and that for him they were always a beleaguered minority locked in a battle with an Oxford academic norm that was something like an ahistorical fusion of empiricism with Aristotle. More shocking still to realize that Collingwood thinks of Russell and Moore as hiding their *recursion* to Victorian mental stuffiness behind their bad moral behavior! (One can only suppose that RGC thought that this was quite different from his own old-time romantic complications . . .)

The serious point here is that, for Collingwood, to ignore history, art, and religion, alongside the real questioning that is Baconian method, was to lock oneself within tautologous circles of willful obscurity. A retreat was made first to the illusion of representational direct realism (as if we could ever claim that thinking leaves things unaffected, without having an extra-cognitive access to the nature of things) and later to an arid logicism unable to account for manifest bodily experiences and unavoidable mental concerns.

One can argue that, for all its sophistication, continental phenomenology exhibited a somewhat parallel perpetuation of again *nineteenth-century* neo-Kantianism in a new guise. An attempt was made to circumvent the primacy of temporal change and of endless Leibnizian spatial perspective by reinstating absolute and dogmatic limits to our understanding—confining us inside "appearances," even though we can never confirm this confinement from within if we remain only within, just as we can never so confirm the solipsism and fixed boundaries of the Kantian categories, or the self-referentiality of logic and language in modern Anglo-Saxon thought.

As time has gone on, of course, the more that both analytic philosophy and phenomenology have deconstructed themselves, the more they have effectively returned to the horizon of Romantic and "idealist" concerns, going behind the hysteria of Victorian positivism and "returns to Kant" (or to Aquinas!) which were always made in the name of rigid order and political (or ecclesiastical) control.

In consequence, with a quarter of the twenty-first century already past, we are returned to the unavoidability of philosophical thought as speculation, or as a kind of hermeneutic of reality, in

Whiteheadian terms, given that "the big questions" of existence, life, the nature of thought, the mystery of free will, the reality of value, and the nature of the ultimate cannot really be avoided. This is because we have to live out, whether as civilizations or as individuals, in some way and in some measure, our answers to them.

Within this new perspective, our categorization of the thinkers of the past, and especially of the recent past, is starting to change. We have tended to suppose that the big division in philosophy is between materialists and realists on the one hand and rationalists and idealists on the other. And yet this way of dividing things up itself supposes that we are essentially detached, knowing subjects looking out on the world as through a sensory window.

Such an assumption is itself a highly modern and recent one, much underscored by Kant, who thought that he had finally arrived at a clear distinction between what the mind itself contributes in knowing and what it receives from sensation. The resulting circle of "correlation" is then supposed to establish "limits" beyond which our categories of understanding, which are only geared to the organization of sensory material arriving from without, no longer apply.

Taken together, the assumption of "detachment" and the "critical" claim to finite limitation constitute the completion of a "turn to the subject" supposed to mark an epochal shift in the entire history of philosophy, and to ensure a new primacy of the epistemological over the metaphysical. The latter may be confined to the regulative, be implied only by the ethical, or be ruled out altogether.

The temptation for the church, when confronted by the skeptical or else human self-vaunting implications of this perspective, has often been to insist instead upon a realism that too much accepts the modern notion of a detached self making no difference to that which it knows, and in consequence is hard put to it to distinguish realism from empiricism and positivism. This was often true of neo-Thomism from the 1860s onwards, which rejected the far subtler alternatives to Kantianism offered by the Schellingian or Coleridge-Newman intellectual trajectories.

What is crucial here is to realize that post-Socratic philosophy itself involved an *ontological* turn to the subject, insofar as, unlike pre-Socratic naturalism, it offered a simultaneous interpretation of both the cosmos and of our mental interiority, referring both to a trans-cosmic principle of transcendence able to account for mind and matter equally, and likewise for both stasis and alteration. This legacy is sustained by Neoplatonism, which by fusing Aristotelian relative objectivity and Platonic relative subjectivity tended further to accentuate the dynamic, living processes in the cosmos, and the dynamic shaping processes of our mind.

We can see the same combination present in Augustine, and should not lose sight of the fact that his greater concern with interiority and spiritual experience long *precedes* Aquinas, who is sometimes troublingly unclear as to just how far our powers of natural intellectual intuition can reach to the Godhead—troubling, as the late Illtyd Trethowan contended, because surely there can be no truth without some remote intuition of God, even of God as he is within himself?

When it comes to the pre-Kantian beginnings of modern philosophy, we need to be alert to ways in which both Francis Bacon and René Descartes, the two philosophers most associated with the "scientific revolution," did not clearly embrace the "detached" attitude of mind that is crucial to the later primacy of epistemology. Bacon stressed that the human mind itself, all its thoughts, and all its artificial works are fully part of nature, while conversely all of nature and our experimental interactions with nature belong to "history." During the twentieth-century perpetuation of British Victorian "speculation," Alfred North Whitehead appealed specifically to Bacon in refusing the "bifurcation" of nature, just as he sustained the Baconian concern to discover generative "processes" in nature, while still linking these to the attraction of ideal "forms."

Bacon's focus upon truth as power and upshot, linked to a concern with form and the light of the mind that Coleridge could later read as Platonic, was far from what we have later come to understand as "empiricism" and proffered more of a "contemplative pragmatism" allied to human synergic participation in eschatological redemption. Bacon's overall sense that we are fully located in a nature imbued with meaning and coherence by God meant that he did not, like John Locke later, really privilege isolated sensory evidence, but rather our entire bodily immersion in a world that directly affects and alters us, and which we directly affect and alter in turn. Again, Whitehead followed suit, along with Collingwood and Michael Oakeshott, other "continuing Victorians." As Oakeshott put it, "What is given in experience is a world, and what is achieved is this given world made more of a world."[1]

When it comes to Descartes, although he is much more guilty of inaugurating a fatal dualism of body and mind, there are crucial mitigations. His *cogito* implies less that being is evidenced by thought, as that thought immediately discloses being, such that they are for us of co-birth, as earlier for Augustine and much later for Ralph Waldo Emerson. Nor is our thinking a matter primarily of representation, or of self-representation as reflection, but of an unfathomable immediacy that grounds our affections as much as our rational analyses. Thus Descartes was able to link the *cogito* to the "passions of the soul" that derive in part from our embodiment.

In the Romantic era, this allowed Maine de Biran to take Cartesianism in an emphatically non-dualist direction. Beyond Descartes, he realized that all our self-awareness is rooted in our bodies, which are at once fully within the world and yet independent of the world from our perspective, since they allow us to move around the world and to control this moving around through our mental inhabitation. Equally, Biran rejected still further the "spectator" view of understanding by insisting that thought begins with the experience of the resistance of other bodies to our own, and the always accompanying counter-resistance of our own bodies, as manifested in the phenomenon of touch. This ensures a concurrence between natural motion, which is nothing but the habituation of patterns of mutual influence, and the process of human thinking, which is an internalized habituation of the same.

This "realism of habit" rather than of Newtonian laws was also, however, for Biran, a "spiritual realism." He pointed out that if the experience of resistance is directly a mental experience, besides a material experience, then this suggests a palpable and yet occult tie between matter on the one hand and spirit on the other. And he further argued, as his thought developed, that if we are affected spiritually and yet materially by other bodies, then it makes sense to suppose that material nature is also at its core somehow also spiritual. This then lets us understand how the compounding of habit in nature, as in us, can be a good compounding, when creatively non-identical

1. Oakeshott, *Experience and Its Modes*, 248.

and flexible in character, and yet disintegrating and bad when habits become lazy and stuck in identical and non-adaptive inertia.

All this implied a non-Darwinian approach to evolution and anticipated later perceptions of nature as composed of exchanges of information, and so as being in some sense in its entirety "alive" and in some sense "thinking."

During the bulk of the nineteenth century the Biranian perspective was developed with great sophistication and further innovation by Félix Ravaisson, whose influence then passed to both Henri Bergson and Maurice Blondel. In the latter case, Ravaisson's view that grace is an integral part of nature, since grace alone accounts for the paradoxical establishment of nature as habit before habit can be formed (habits being by definition formed realities), composes part of the background to Blondel's integralist insistence that all of nature is involved in a natural drive to the supernatural, since its lure is always hovering.

In the two cases of revived and deepened Baconian and Cartesian legacies, we see that modern thought has not necessarily been caught within the collusive alternatives of either rationalism or empiricism. Indeed, we can see that in some ways these were always *conservative* and often religiously motivated programs, intended to restrict the Renaissance realization of mutability and the unlimited capacities of human creative transformation. Idealism and rationalism may allow that knowing alters what is known, or that there only exists for certain what is known, but it tends to try to confine this alteration within pre-given patterns of logic and *a priori* categorization, always subordinating the operations of will and of poetic transformation.

By contrast, "spiritual realism," whether in its French version or in its Anglo-Saxon equivalents (Coleridge, Emerson, C. S. Pierce, T. H. Green, Whitehead, Collingwood, etc.), at once hangs onto our commonsense experience that both mind and matter are equally real, and yet also allows much more radical and real mutations and creative human interventions.

A third parallel strand of reflection along these lines occurs in the German Romantic modification of Leibniz, freeing his vision of real interactive natural spiritual monads from both predetermination and logical fixity—above all in the case of Schelling, whose thought was partially incorporated by Coleridge into the authentic "Platonic-empiricist" Anglo-Saxon tradition. Eventually, these three (besides Russian Sophiology, in the Germanic wake) were joined by the Japanese Kyoto school, which synthesized aspects of European spiritual realism with Asiatic thought.

Two further points stand out here. First, while the modern, post-scientific "turn to the subject" is sustained, it remains for these currents much more traditionally ontological in character and tends to altogether *sidestep* Kantian epistemology, even if many Kantian insights (especially concerning the metaphysical over-extension of non-intuitive reason) remain fruitful for spiritually realist currents of thought. This is because the primordially bodily experience of being in the world, just like our linked primordially linguistic experience of the same, does not allow for any sifting of sensory evidence coming from without and mental categorization coming from within. Our body senses always from within through "self-affection," while its organization of our sensing is always already begun and experienced as also passively received from without, as much as actively organized from our own mental imposition. Here touch is once more paradigmatic (as already for Aristotle): We are only passively touched because we are in some degree actively touching. And again this is as much a spiritual, as a material exchange.

The second point is the way in which spiritually realist traditions sustain a link to the Renaissance (manifest also in the Italian spiritual realism of Antonio Rosmini), which dubious piety has often sought to suppress in its exaltation of epistemology. Despite his considerable implication in this suppression, Descartes sustained the notion that even God is *causa sui,* or self-creating, as much as he is just "there"—an idea present in Nicholas of Cusa and transmitted to him originally from Plotinus through Eriugena and Eckhart. In the later unfolding of French Spiritualism in Bergson, Blondel, and the remarkable philosopher and stylist Louis Lavelle (whom some now judge equal, or superior, to Heidegger) all understand human spiritual acting in terms of our participation in this primordial creativity. Since this is but the highest manifestation of all of nature's sharing in the divine creative capacity, this also ensures our participation in all natural things that we know and an overcoming of our distanced alienation from them as illusory.

Aimé Forest (1898–1983) is significant above all because he stood, like the later Maurice Blondel, at the intersection of the French spiritualist legacy with the French Thomistic revival, whose main exponents were Étienne Gilson and Jacques Maritain. He fully embraced the realism of these two authors and yet he had a keener sense, as witnessed in the current book, of the arguments that might seem to favor idealism. Above all, he realized that we do not experience reality bit by bit in an empiricist fashion, but always with an intimation of its patterned coherence—like Oakeshott's emphasis on the linkage of experience with "world." This is strongly attuned with the Biranian view that our very physical interactions with the external world fall into temporally narrative and geographically extensive (both witnessed and inferred) stretches of linked occurrences, such that we are never simply piecing together bits of isolated information. And in keeping with Descartes, rather than Bacon, our insertion as thinkers within the world means that from the very outset we have an immediate intuitive grasp of our very widest circumstances—that existence and thinking and the encounter with otherness all fall singly together (as again, for both Augustine and Emerson).

For Forest, the fact that we only know by construing the entirety of reality as coherent, and that we do so in an active manner that is as much physically external as mentally internal, can strongly tempt us to go in the fully idealist direction of supposing that all of reality is our creation and a mental projection or construction. Indeed, this is almost for him a necessary temptation, a kind of dark purgation that the contemporary philosopher must inevitably undergo.

However, this temptation is halted (as it was even halted for the later J. G. Fichte) by the further realization that we never get to the end of our spiritual-physical exploration and experimentation. Reality always exceeds our mental grasp, and ever new depths later appear even in the formulations that we think we have already fully grasped. For this reason, we have to realize that we are only, after all, thinking "after things," and that even our new artificial and cultural inventions depend upon a receptive inspiration, anticipating new realities to come in the future.

This purgation and awakening make us see the primacy after all of encounter, and of the existential over the intellectual, in tune with both Gilson and Maritain. However, Forest is distinctive in refusing to let go of the element of truth in the idealist perspective: namely that we do not simply "bump into being," much less into a sheerly existential being, but always in some measure with a being that we to some degree directly experience as an integrated, structured whole, only comprehensible by our thought that internally resonates with what it finds without—as for Coleridge's reading of Bacon. This is what Forest meant by talking in his eventually published doctoral thesis about "concrete being" in Aquinas.

Read this way, what Thomistic thought implies is that we do, indeed, co-experience external reality as also the unfolding discovery and action of our internal spirit, but that, because we cannot *fully* create what we come to see, we have to also regard this reality as deriving from an infinite mind in unreachable excess of our own. This is rather different from an induction back to God as cause, according to the Five Ways, though it may be coherent with Aquinas's deeper insights. It is rather reminiscent of Biran's contention that if matter acts upon our spirit, then this is because it is the vehicle of a deeper spirit in nature, and evidence of a grace-leading and infusing presence beyond nature.

Hence, for Forest to know God as author of created existence is also to know him at once as the immanent thinker of this existence.

And in another way also, Forest qualifies some more typical Thomistic stances. For him, realism is less a matter of proof than of a kind of mystical experience. For one cannot rationally convince the obstinate idealist like Hegel that we may not have in some way already come to the "end" of the logically unfolding human rational process. Nor can we convince the really obstinate Kantian skeptic that we are not trapped in the awareness only of appearances.

The same applies today to phenomenologists who see phenomenology as all of philosophy. Despite the sophisticated reading of Descartes by Michel Henry and Jean-Luc Marion on the lines indicated above, they still want to make an arbitrary ontological distinction between the immediate affective "inside" of reality and the supposedly dubious mediated encounters with its "outside," with the latter regarded as "domineering"—as if touch could not be as much art as technology. Yet ultimately this phenomenological stance only repeats more subtly the detached dualism of the epistemological stance.

Today, this is arguably challenged by the revival of the Biranian tradition in key Catholic thinkers like Andrea Bellantone and Emmanuel Gabellieri. No duality of internal "real" phenomena over against a kind of gnostically fallen ontological husk can really be compatible with the primacy of reciprocal bodily encounter in Biran, Ravaisson, and their successors.

But nor can this encounter be seen as residually "representational" if the bifurcation of nature is rejected. Even the Aristotelian theory of knowledge "by identity of form" is not enough, if one wishes to affirm an Augustinian intentionality that in some way reaches through grasped intellectual form back to real materialized form or to pure spiritual bodies. It is at that point that we can only think of thinking as a kind of pure and mysterious ecstasy that we must trust if we wish to reach out to any thing or to any person in love. (This ecstatic reach of spirit to concrete being as such clearly distances Forest from Maréchal and Rahner's Kantian *aprioristic* understanding of natural spirit as merely aspirational.)

It is just this that Forest means by our "consent to being." Simply in order to know anything at all we must trust it, allowing its presence beyond us by a kind of leap of faith. It thereby turns out that (as for Pierce or Oakeshott) there is no *uncommitted* mode of understanding. At this juncture, Forest was consistently trying to integrate more of Augustine into the Thomistic perspective—to allow that our experience of ourselves as spiritual and thinking is as primordial as our experience of Being, including ourselves as existing. Augustine was therefore right to insist upon his encounter with God in his own depths. But these depths are not a sort of exclusive enclave lurking behind our window-box gaze upon nature. Instead, as later for Goethe, Emerson, and Whitehead, these depths within us are also the depths of nature herself, which we inhabit immediately. Yet not such as to refuse external encounter, or to reduce it, "phenomenologically," to self-affection, which is really another mode of idealism, falsely claiming an identity with God already here on earth. The point is much rather that we encounter only *ourselves* also as other—thus for Augustine as arriving from the past and the anticipated future in the present—and that this encounter occurs only *simultaneously* with the entire remembered and anticipated history of our encounter with finite others and their *own* hidden depths.

Like the depths of everything in the Biranian tradition, just because we meet them consciously from without, they must themselves be speaking to us from a mysterious seclusion from within.

Forest insisted that this interiority of everything was ultimately God, who alone has created and fully grasps all of reality. But he also thought that we can only "consent" to this because of the equal Augustinian mystery of our own spiritual capacity to consent, arising from our own depths which are at once and equally existential, intellectual, and creative. To consent in this way is to become aware of the "spiritual bonds" that form the topic of Forest's final and most complex treatise: the *Essai sur les forms du lien spirituel.* We both traverse and constitute the bond of knowing and being, which is analogically akin to the ultimately spiritual bonds that pertain between each and every thing and that, with equal mystery, hold every existing thing together in a kind of figure of the incarnation or (for Blondel after Leibniz) of the transubstantiated elements of the Eucharist.

Aimé Forest is therefore one of many kindred thinkers who can, in the twenty-first century, lead us away from the sterility both of mainline modern (or semi-modern?) anti-metaphysical reflection and of return to a merely fantasized pre-modern that ignores its own post-Socratic anticipations of a genuinely modern, Renaissance concern with both a moving cosmos and an acting humanity in their inseparable cooperation under God.

John Milbank

Acknowledgments

TRANSLATION OF A HIGHLY original thinker is a difficult enough enterprise. It is rendered even more difficult when the thinker is as subtle a philosopher as Aimé Forest. Even a so-called straightforward translation, which this one attempts to be, necessarily entails a degree of interpretation, if only to ensure that the limpid clarity of the original is maintained. I am particularly indebted, therefore, to Lucien Pelletier, a francophone philosopher at the Université de Sudbury (in Ontario), who so generously took of his time to scrutinize the manuscript.

I owe thanks also to Graeme Ward, who helped me with the translation and sourcing of the Latin and Greek phrases scattered throughout Forest's text.

I am grateful also to my editor, Robin Parry, for his reliable support and advice throughout the project, and his peerless editing towards the end.

Introduction

AIMÉ FOREST (1898–1983) WAS a French metaphysical philosopher and historian of medieval philosophy, a lifelong academic who spent most of his career in relative obscurity as a professor in the Faculty of Letters and Human Sciences at the University of Montpellier. *Du consentement à l'être*, published in 1936, was his first book, and now, to the best of my knowledge, the first of his books to appear in English translation. Various factors have led to the neglect of his enormous significance for philosophy, even in his native France: an originality and independence that placed him on the margins of the main currents of French philosophy, the highly demanding nature of his writing, and not least what the editor of the French reedition of this book describes as "his modesty, and what must be recognized as the grandeur of his soul, more yet his humility."[1]

Consent to Being is a very short book, yet a very ambitious one, undertaking nothing less than the task of resurrecting metaphysical thought in our time. Although its subject is metaphysics, it offers no system purporting to encompass all that is, but instead eschews extension in favor of a tightly gathered intensity. It might seem a very dense and difficult, or better put, a very concise and subtle book; yet it is nevertheless also very clear, even limpid in its style. The greater challenge for the translator, with a few exceptions, is not the original French vocabulary and syntax, but being confident one has sufficiently grasped the conceptual argument in order to translate it accurately.

1. Forest, *Du consentement à l'être*, preface by Philippe-Marie Margelidon, 11.

Before saying more about that argument, let us briefly situate Forest within his intellectual milieu. The subject of his doctoral thesis at the Sorbonne was the metaphysics of the concrete according to Thomas Aquinas, which he had to defend against the "barrage" of criticism levelled against it by one of the leading figures of French idealist philosophy, Léon Brunschvicg, who presided over his examining jury.[2] Brunschvicg, as well as other twentieth-century French idealists such as Jules Lagneau, Octave Hamelin, and Jules Lachelier, who will likely be unknown to most English-speaking readers, are cited and engaged by Forest in *Consent to Being*. Well-versed as he was in the neo-Kantian idealism that then reigned in French academic philosophy, and as we shall see, not entirely unsympathetic to its approach, he nevertheless placed himself generally within the horizon of Catholic "neo-Thomism," though not in the sense of belonging to a school. While the influence of Thomas is evident in what could be called the "spiritual realism" of *Consent to Being*, so too is the inspiration of Plato, Augustine, Pascal, and Maine de Biran.

The opening sentence of *Consent to Being* identifies a problem that at first sight might seem of interest only to a particular category of professional philosopher: "Metaphysical thought always presents itself under the form of extreme abstraction."[3] As we enter into Forest's work, however, it becomes apparent that his goal of saving metaphysics from abstraction is tantamount to saving the whole of philosophy and human thought itself. Forest begins in the first chapter by turning on its head the conventional opposition between the concrete realism of empirical science and the "abstractions" of metaphysical philosophy. His argument—that it is actually the scientific understanding that loses itself in abstraction, while metaphysics, properly understood and carried out, is what truly takes us to the heart of concrete being—is, in its own way, as radical as Heidegger's famous "science does not think."[4] Forest identifies two philosophical

2. See Forest, *Du consentement à l'être*, preface by Philippe-Marie Margelidon, 8. The exact title of Forest's doctoral thesis was "La structure métaphysique du concret selon saint Thomas d'Aquin."

3. Forest, *Consent to Being*, 1.

4. See especially Heidegger, *What Is Called Thinking*, Part I, Lecture 1: "Science itself does not think, and cannot think—which is its good fortune, here meaning the assurance of its own appointed course."

paths to the salvation of thought from the abstract limitations of the scientific understanding, each one the subject of a different chapter: the "idealist conversion" (chapter 2) and the realist "consent to being" (chapter 3). While giving the idealist conversion its full due, it is the consent to being that he identifies as the more promising path to the heart of reality.

The path, or to use the term on which Forest insists, the *method* of consent to being consists in the prolonging of objective thought, of what could also be called thoughtful experience, beyond the point where it tends to arrest itself prematurely, to settle for clinging to partial, limited, abstract determinations of the real. This arresting of thought falls short of *being*, and by the same token, also falls short of grasping *beings* in their intimate singularity. For Forest, attaining to being and to beings is not a matter of "either-or" but "both-and." As he puts it, "There is . . . a kind of 'reversal from for to against,' or to employ Hegelian language, after that of Pascal, we will speak of the process of *Aufhebung*, by which what is gone beyond is not repudiated, but found again on another level."[5]

Forest likens the overcoming of the tendency of thought to arrest itself prematurely in its contemplation of reality as a kind of "victory" of thought over itself.[6] There is much that is compelling in *Consent to Being*, but it is particularly this victory of thought on which I would like to focus in these introductory remarks. This notion of thought achieving a victory over itself might at first appear paradoxical. What Forest means is that the natural impulse of thought to know reality is arrested prematurely by a desire for certainty that tempts it to cling to the abstract determinations of the scientific understanding. It thereby misses its natural destiny of rising from beings to their source in the absolute principle of being which solicits the ascent of thought. Thought need only remain determinedly faithful and attentive to the original impulse [*élan*], prolonging it sufficiently so as to enter truly into the path of metaphysics. Then the apparent paradox of thought conquering itself becomes a matter of thought fulfilling its natural destiny. In an essay written around the same time as *Consent to Being*, Forest offers his

5. Forest, *Consent to Being*, 61.

6. Forest, *Consent to Being*, 66.

most explicit understanding of what metaphysical thought, and indeed philosophical thought as a whole, truly is:

> Philosophy has always experienced great difficulties in seeking to define itself in its orientation, development, and progress. But the ideal it undertakes to attain, realized in very diverse ways, remains most often that proposed by Plato. The philosopher, as distinguished from the sophist or the politician, is the dialectician. . . . Dialectic is defined only by the effort to climb up to principles, whatever the process thanks to which one might get there. . . . In this Platonic inspiration, philosophy presents itself as the search for the principles, not that this search is indifferent in some way to the truth it obtains, but because it is a universal putting into question, and as has been said "the search for a first truth." Philosophy will appear from then on, in the proper sense of the word, as a *method;* let us understand by this a quest, the effort to attain an end, or simply the study, or again if you wish, the "setting out on the path" of the truth.[7]

According to Forest's interpretation of Plato, philosophy itself, at its height, is a method, an entry into the dialectic that take us up towards first principles. This helps us to understand why Forest's rescue of metaphysics does not entail a *system*, and why he often characterizes the path of consent to being as a *method*, which is also an essay, a venture, a pursuit—and not a treatise with a series of conclusions. The dialectic into which *Consent to Being* leads us entails reflection on the perennial dilemma of the one and the many, being and beings, unity and multiplicity. What is perhaps most striking about the way that Forest addresses this ultimate question of metaphysics is his use of what he calls the "doctrine of analogy" (most fully developed in chapter 4), which he apparently draws from Thomas Aquinas. This doctrine makes possible a remarkable "proof" of God in *Consent to*

7. Forest, "La recherche philosophique," an appendix included in *Du consentement à l'être*, 87. (The translation is mine, as are the other quotations from French texts in this introduction.) This essay, originally published by Forest in the *Revue thomiste* in 1937, offers a most helpful further unpacking of central, though largely implicit, themes in *Consent to Being*. I will draw from it frequently in these introductory remarks.

Being—Aliquid est, ergo Deus est[8]—not in the sense of a "first cause" but of a proportional relation. More than this, it makes possible, according to Forest, an understanding of human participation in the divine life: "Thus, the doctrine of analogy doesn't only establish in an objective vision the proportional unity of the being given to us and of God; it recognizes also the analogical unity of the act by which we carry ourselves towards being, in seeking to possess it, and the act by which God creates it."[9]

Consent to Being never ceases to be a rigorous work of metaphysical philosophy, and in thus adhering faithfully to the philosophical dialectic it at the same time demonstrates what Forest, in his account of his own philosophical development, affirmed as the agreement between the metaphysical vision and the religious affirmation.[10] Both call for an "attitude of soul" that amounts to a sort of conversion.[11]

In what does this attitude of soul consist? "Fidelity and courage, attention and consent, these are the spiritual conditions of the conquest of philosophical truth."[12] According to Forest, these are the intellectual virtues of the thinker whom Plato designates in the *Phaedrus* as worthy to be called a "lover of wisdom," a *philosopher.* Forest then notes that after this praise, Plato's Socrates goes on to indicate that there might be something more that surpasses even this ideal: "It could be, he says, that the one who seeks the truth will be led 'to greater things by a more divine impulse.'"[13]

Thus, to the intellectual virtues of fidelity and courage, attention and consent, Forest adds one more—purity of heart. And here he invokes Augustine: "God is known by those who have a pure heart and the heart is purified only by faith."[14] The prolongation of the

8. "Something is, therefore God is." Forest, *Consent to Being,* 47.

9. Forest, *Consent to Being,* 72.

10. See Forest, "Itinéraire philosophique."

11. Forest, "La recherche philosophique," 88, 113.

12. Forest, "La recherche philosophique," 114.

13. Forest, "La recherche philosophique," 114. See Plato's *Phaedrus,* 278 C, 279 A.

14. Forest, "La recherche philosophique," 94. He refers here to Augustine's *Confessions,* VI, 4, 6.

natural impulse of thought towards beings so that it can ascend to the absolute of being, or what Forest calls the method of "consent to being," thus involves a moral preparation that cannot do without the healing or purifying power of faith.

In the final, fifth chapter of Forest's book, entitled "The Spiritual Possession of Being," he states that once philosophy recognizes that the "essential metaphysical idea" is the idea of "orientation," then through this idea "philosophy fulfills its whole task, and without drawing on resources other than those proper to it, raises itself at least to the naming of the first love."[15] This rather cryptic reference to love is the only one found in *Consent to Being.* Perhaps this reticence is attributable to Forest's concern to contain the metaphysical argument within the "resources proper to it." He is in other writings more forthcoming about the immense significance of the experience of love for his thought, emphasizing that it is essential to that attitude of soul entailed in the method of consent to being. In *La recherche philosophique,* he notes that love is the "motor" of the Platonic dialectic, and more than this, "completes it in a sense."[16] Indeed, that spiritual possession of being, which is the culmination of the method of consent he is proposing, "will be love at the same time it is vision."[17]

The full import of the experience of love for Forest is found in his very personal account of his life in philosophy, entitled *Nos promesses encloses*, a kind of reprise of Dante's *Vita Nuova,* in which the author comes to comprehend *l'intelleto d'amore.*[18] Here there is no reticence about the significance of what Forest calls "illuminating love" for both the metaphysical vision and the religious affirmation: "Love is first. I do not see what we can place above it, without a sort of failing that we cannot accept without denying our very selves."[19] In this poignant reflection on the love he experienced with his wife, Jeanne, whom he never loved *en dehors de* [outside] his intellectual search, and with their two children, Michel and Dominique, he

15. Forest, *Consent to Being,* 73.

16. Forest, "La recherche philosophique," 112.

17. Forest, "La recherche philosophique," 112.

18. "The intelligence of love." Forest, *Nos promesses encloses,* 341. See Dante, *La Vita Nuova,* XIX.

19. Forest, *Nos promesses encloses,* 172.

testifies to the association of love and thought that undergirds the flourishing of both: "Those who love each other enter, one through the other, into the mystery of charity. The penetration of philosophic thought is now in this affinity. The soul interrogates itself and recognizes itself in the progress which it knows to follow. *Factus eram mihi magna quaestio.*"[20]

A Note About Notes

This is a short book, as noted above, partly because Forest's style of thought aimed at intensity rather than extension, at going to the heart of the matter rather than getting bogged down in explanatory detail. To this end, in this essay, he eschews conceptual digressions and marginal explanations. His text also, as was to be the case in all his subsequent works, does without footnotes, except in the case of longer extract quotations. Where there are footnotes in the original French text, they are included as they appear there. As an author, Forest had the good fortune to be able to assume that shorter quotations, of which there are few, would be familiar enough to his readers that no citation would be needed, though he usually makes clear who is being quoted. In keeping with Forest's own desire to avoid scholarly clutter, these remain without footnotes in this translation. Forest was also able to assume a knowledge of ancient languages on the part of his readers, and he does intersperse a number of Latin and Greek phrases that are significant to his argument. For each of these, I have included a footnote with my translation and have cited the source in such a way that the interested reader can find the phrase in either a Latin or Greek edition, or in any English translation.

20. Forest, *Nos promesses encloses*, 341. These are the closing words of Forest's memoir. The Latin phrase, "I have become to myself a huge question," is from Augustine's *Confessions*, IV, 9. The memoir was written late in his life, after yet another of his memorial visits to Oradour-sur-glane, the site of a massacre carried out by a Waffen-SS company in June 1944 as a reprisal for French resistance activity in the area. Among those murdered were their two children, his sister, and other members of their extended family.

1

About Metaphysical Explication

METAPHYSICAL THOUGHT ALWAYS PRESENTS itself to us under the form of extreme abstraction. It therefore always seems to hold us far away from the being that it wants to help us know, and often the questions it raises remain in our eyes, in great measure, arbitrary and vain. This is because the significance of these problems is only truly perceived when the spirit[1] places itself, following a spontaneous movement, in that attitude of universality that metaphysics demands we adopt. We reflect, for example, on the relations between the ideal and the real, on the meaning of contingency; but in order for these very questions to make sense, we must, by an effort of abstraction, recognize the characteristics by which the given being appears to us contingent, at the level of an original reflection. But it is not in a way that is absolutely immediate and direct that thought is going to

1. The French *esprit*, used throughout by Forest, can be translated as "mind" or "spirit." The distinction sometimes depends on context, but rather than risk any undue narrowing of Forest's meaning, I have translated his *esprit* always as "spirit." The more religious overtones of the word are certainly in keeping with the direction of his thought. *Consent to Being* was, moreover, a seminal work within the twentieth-century French philosophical movement that called itself the *philosophie de l'esprit*—that is, the "philosophy of the spirit."

consider those aspects of reality whose explication can only take a metaphysical form. Thus, for reflections of this type to cease appearing to us as the result of who knows what kind of purely logical artifice, it would be necessary to follow the movement of thought that, starting from the simplest experience, leads us to them. It would be necessary to recover the "natural order" that philosophy most often, so Pascal tells us, has not known how to keep. Metaphysical thought should come to pose the problems in the same order in which thought discerns them; this ordered progression would thereby constitute the synthesis to which philosophy wants to raise itself. But is it possible to follow in this way the advance of thought and to recover its diverse implications within an absolutely finished order? Philosophers have often despaired of this, and we are not thinking of taking up entirely such an audacious task. We are setting out, at least, to follow the first steps of philosophical thought. Metaphysical explication can indeed only have an intelligible character if we show in the first place what natural and basic method helps us grasp the characteristics of the real for which it wants to offer rational explanation. We would like to attempt to follow the ideal genesis and, so to speak, witness the birth of metaphysical thought.

When thought undertakes to comprehend the given, it begins by neglecting certain aspects of it; explication only appears possible to us on the condition that it be limited. Those elements that we don't take into account are isolated by an effort of thought; we do not say they lack reality, we simply affirm that they are not the object of our current consideration. The real upon which our consideration bears will therefore be in some respect abstract, and the sciences are the result of this abstraction. They will never get to the point of explaining rationally the totality of characteristics manifested by the real. Explication, in effect, can only be built up by leaning on the recognition of an anterior element it presupposes. For example, if we are seeking to characterize life by finality, we must admit that the elements it succeeds in organizing in a synthesis are themselves given; we are obliged to have recourse to them in order to construct beyond [them] a richer, more complete representation. Mechanism itself, if we consider it as a simpler genus of being, already assumes that the real is constituted according to genera, and it is this very notion of being, or of genera, that we are leaving aside in seeking to determine the laws of mechanism. The sciences thus always bear on particular and limited aspects of being; it is this abstraction that is the origin of their distinction. It is the foundation that supports the entirety of scientific knowledge and renders possible its progress.

One will note, it is true, that thought is able to go past the level of real existence and consider truths that are valuable for the order of possibles. We are ourselves, in this case, at the starting point of the ideal genesis of truths, we dominate them entirely, it seems, in the act by which we constitute them. But doesn't it nevertheless remain that the possible enters into the genera of being, that there is an order of possible truths at the moment that thought constitutes them? That is what we must still assume and that we thus, in a certain way, leave outside the explication itself. Applying itself to building up progressively the network of intelligible or true relations, thought can succeed in making appear the novelty of the results it produces in its reasonings; yet this same novelty will only be possible for thought because being lends itself in this way to its movement under the form of the organization of possibles. There will perpetually be possibles about which we won't be able to say whether they are anterior to the movement of thought, or the result only of its predictive reasonings, but being includes them, and this is what we must admit, without yet explaining it, at the starting point of our constructions. Thus the attitude of science is always provisory and incomplete in some respect, it is made to be exceeded. Science habituates us to being satisfied with certainties that are partial but rigorous, its value in our eyes perhaps coming not from the universality of the object on which it bears but from the absolute rigor with which its results are reached. It gives us in the explication it offers the sentiment of totality, so near to that of infinity, when we consider not the end to be attained, nor the nature of the known object, which always in certain ways escapes our grasp, but the rigor of the method and the perfection of the proof, which, in the terms they are presented, leave nothing more to be sought.

Let us suppose, however, that we are seeking to comprehend without excluding anything and without always referring ourselves, from reduction to reduction, to what itself is never taken as such for object in the analysis that the scientific understanding is able to effect. This requirement is perhaps chimerical, it is not sure that we would find any resource within ourselves permitting us to fulfill it.

Still, it is the case that it appears in a natural way in the spontaneity of our thought. Let us not consider for the moment the difficulties that thought can encounter in its effort to penetrate the intelligence of the real, let us simply try to follow the reach of its ambitions, the scope of its aim. Why wouldn't we go past the boundaries that always present themselves before the aspirations of science? Why wouldn't we be able to come to a comprehension that excludes nothing and presupposes nothing, and how would we not attempt to extend the reach of explication back to the final point? In this way, alongside positive science there appears another type of research and new endeavors. Because if the sciences focus on the determined aspects of the real, there is a notion underlying each of these partial abstractions, and which thus exceeds them all; this is the idea of being. The progress of thought allows us to discern it, present itself under each of the objects we can consider in the order of the possible, as well as in that of the real. At the starting point of each of the sciences we are already giving ourselves the idea of being, without bringing actual consideration to bear on it in a methodical way. The results obtained by the scientific understanding thus only have the value of being and truth through the reality of the being implied in their very expression, but that remains beyond what science determines. In this sense one can say that the reality of science is relative to that of metaphysics; scientific abstraction still recognizes the reality of what surpasses it and that it implies; it cannot hold as exclusive, as though sufficient unto themselves, the aspects of the real whose knowledge is determined.

Metaphysics therefore intends to take as object of study the very reality that is presupposed in the sciences and that gives them their truth value. It defines itself first by its requirement of universality, it doesn't know what could limit it in its effort of explication, and from its starting point, it is the totality of the real it would like to possess. It doesn't yet ask itself by what method it could attain this goal, but it recognizes at least that the explication it wants to arrive at wouldn't even be begun if it left something outside its grasp, it if bore only on a particular aspect of the real. Metaphysics would like, if it is possible, to comprehend without having the feeling that not everything is mastered, and that there remains an unexplored residue, a last zone where perhaps all the obscurity of the real is gathered. Perhaps what there is of the unintelligible in the world is being progressively driven out, pushed away by the successive conquests of the positive sciences, but while remaining on the level of those sciences, we are never assured that all the obscurity isn't concentrating itself in who knows what mystery of the thing or of being, and that from there it won't come anew to invade the regions where we thought to have established the truth in all its rigor. Thought is thus only obeying the instinct that defines its nature and following the rigor of its principles, near to nature, when it pushes its own demands forward, supposes that they can all be realized, and instead of seeking like the positive sciences to limit the domain of the irrational, tries to give itself a world become, so to speak, transparent to thought in the perfection of its actual presence. Metaphysical reflection thus appears as a natural consequence of the spontaneous progress of our thought, on which the real itself imposes its movement. We raise ourselves up to the determination of the new problems that are offered to us, led by the effort of discernment leading us to take hold of the most general characteristics of the object offered to us. But this methodical movement isn't completed without a quite manifest change of level. Metaphysical thought forbids itself from being satisfied by the indefinitely expanding conquest of results each of which would remain partial and limited; the provisory character of the explication would simply show that thought hasn't been faithful to itself, that its movement isn't conformed to its original aims. The distinction between metaphysics and the positive sciences thus comes from the fact that we cannot consider, in one identical attitude of thought, the particular aspects of the real and the unity of being found implied in them in a varied way. But if this new orientation of thought and of philosophic research sometimes appears difficult to us, how could we renounce committing ourselves to this direction? We would have to take for the things themselves each of the objects of scientific knowledge, arresting the movement of our thought at these determinations, these achieved abstractions, in the aftermath of which we will never have being itself. Thus science is built up and takes its reality-value only on this condition, that the objects fixed in its formulas and laws appear relative to a beyond on which metaphysics rightly brings its consideration to bear.

The originality of metaphysical thought is now going to appear to us in a way inverse and complementary to the former way. Far from distancing us from concrete reality, it, on the contrary, implies it and comprehends it within itself by its very focus, in the highest abstraction, on universal being. The sciences doubtless focus on a reality that in itself is concrete, but they never consider it according to its ultimate characteristics, which are the foundation of the singular perfections and are tied to the idea of being, taken in all its universality. This is what we must try to demonstrate by clarifying what we mean by this term, concrete reality. We might think first of saying that the concrete is the entire determination of the concept. The idea of the human comprehends only those general characteristics open to all individuals, but a being considered in a singular way has actually to be made up of the ensemble of characteristics about which I can always pronounce myself in his regard. I'm not always obliged to give a response to a question posed about the nature of an abstract, precisely because the nature of the abstract is that of the incomplete and, so to speak, the provisory, and it is no longer like that of a concrete being all of whose characteristics are determined and specified in the existence in which it finds itself placed. Perhaps we could therefore go to the concrete reality by determining entirely the characteristics that the abstract leaves in their incompleteness, their virtuality. But how could this totality be reached? Doubtless the concrete is the complete determination, but we must now add that this complete determination is still infinite. We will never come to exhaust the series of characteristics that we can attribute to a concrete reality, it remains beyond its determinations, that is, it is their source and not their sum. The concrete is thus, following Bergson's expression, that infinite "that lends itself to an estimation that is indivisible and an enumeration that is inexhaustible." The abstract itself entails a certain infinity, in the sense that we can always vary the series of singular things to which it applies, and that it is liable to being suited to all of them; so it is thereby, at least in a virtual manner, made up of the infinity of characteristics we can attribute to it. But it is not in this sense that we can say of concrete being that it is infinite. It actually envelops an infinity of determinations that proceed from it, that is, from what it is in fact and not what it is open to becoming as the form of a multiplicity of subjects. The least of the concrete realities offered to me is rich in a diversity I cannot come to exhaust, at the same time that it excludes all others, brought back to itself, so to say, in the simple unity of its actual being. We must therefore come to link in a metaphysical manner the idea of singularity to that of infinity. That is what we mean in affirming that the concrete is of another nature than the abstract, that it is not the indefinitely expanded sum of abstract notions. This is doubtless what the most immediate experience suggests, at the same time as it happens to confirm the rigor of the analysis. Let us say in fact that the concrete is in relation to the abstract like a beyond, and this is what we understand by the existence of the thing. Let us place ourselves before our direct experience. What do we mean when affirming that this tree I see shaken by the rain exists as a concrete reality? All that we can say about it appears detached by our spirit's examination from a reality simpler and richer, but that we cannot succeed in fixing in itself. All these characteristics, on the contrary, are only given to the extent that they refer to the existence in which they come together. This [existence] is like the synthetic tie that makes of it a unity, it is beyond the multiplicity of the elements that it unifies in the simplicity of its act.

The orientation of philosophical research towards the truths the possession of which it wants to assure us therefore assumes, first of all, what we will call the sense of the concrete. Metaphysical thought is as if awakened by this observation, the import of which moreover is difficult to determine correctly, that we are in the presence of a universe made up of singular perfections. It presupposes first that we know how to give to this recognition of the concrete its full relief and that the spirit allows itself to be guided by it in some way. Let us allow to appear before our eyes any evocation familiar to us, any image that we well know is going to be present as if in the background of our consciousness. It's not necessary that this direct impression of reality be connected with any striking event. Maybe it was an impression destined to be fleeting, but in which the character of the real has manifested itself to us with particular clarity. In an unexpected way, things appeared to us to have an intimacy,[2] an original significance,

2. *Intimité* could be translated in a more literary way as "innermost depth" or "interiority." But Forest's very deliberate use of the word where, as he says a little later in this chapter, there is no "better term" to convey his meaning, requires, I think, the English word "intimacy." Indeed, the sense of private or secret mutual relatedness, which the English term conveys, is appropriate, as shall see, in light of Forest's emphasis on the mutual connection between spirit and being.

and we know settings where we understood what was the presence of ourselves to ourselves in the midst of intensely real things. But what is this significance we are thereby invited to recognize in the real? What makes things to be themselves always remains beyond what we can express of them in a definite representation. It is thus that the singular reality implies something other than the sum of the determinations of the understanding. Beyond their particular characteristics, we discern the unity that constitutes them, the infinity they manifest, and the reality of the singular existence still remains irreducible to objectivity for our thought.

Consequently, the movement of thought by which we would like to situate ourselves on the level where things appear concrete is of the same nature as that which puts us in the presence of the universality of being. Because this universal envelops all the modalities of being, far from excluding, it comprehends within itself the final characteristics that make being concrete. Concrete reality doubtless surpasses all that can be the object of a defined and determined thought. But this infinity is the very character of being; it [infinity] finds in it [being] its foundation, and it is on the universality of being, beyond all partial abstraction, that metaphysical thought wants to focus. Therefore, just as metaphysics has appeared to us as the science of the universal, so we can say it has for its proper object the study of concrete reality. Through this wish to exclude none of the characteristics necessary for taking account of the concrete, it finds itself in the presence of the object it should be analyzing: being in its universality. Thus the orientation towards the concrete is already the appetite for the universal, and to this in a certain way our richest experience already witnesses. Let's try again to situate ourselves in the presence of one of the realities that appeared to us under their concrete aspect, because our thought was more receptive, more open, or because a spontaneous accord prepared us better to grasp their meaning. We want thus to attach ourselves to these aspects of the real, to try to penetrate all their perfection, though we really know it's inexhaustible, and by this very attaching of ourselves to the singularity of things, we are far from distancing ourselves from the other aspects of the real; we regain them all, so to speak, in the being in which they communicate. Thus, to the extent that our understanding of being becomes purer, our attachment to singular realities becomes livelier. We divine something of the perfection they envelop, we no longer risk allowing ourselves to hold to an exclusive attachment, which would divert us from the universality of being or its principle. The approaches of metaphysics thus appear to us to converge. It doesn't want to leave anything outside its grasp, neither from the side of universality nor from the side of the intimacy of the singular. It orients itself towards the concrete in the same movement that carries it beyond abstract determinations, the object of the positive sciences. Metaphysics directs itself at the same time towards the simple and the all; it would like to grasp in the being the whole foundation of the characteristics it manifests, to leave nothing outside its grip, that is to say, to go by way of a universal vision to what we will call, failing a better term, the intimacy of things. These two approaches are not opposed, on the contrary, they are in accord and even imply each other. They are within the continuity of the impulse that has permitted us to define metaphysics as the demand of a thinking that wants to take the explication up to the final term, never to consider the object solely under the aspect of the limited determinations. It doesn't seek to comprehend by a method of reduction, it doesn't intend to limit in any way what must be supposed for an explication to be possible. In a word, the distinctive task of metaphysics is to reconquer being above the determinations.

Metaphysical problems are thus not the object of an artificial reflection, thought cannot not encounter them when it wants simply to be faithful to itself, when it refuses to arrest the movement that leads it at the same time towards universal being and towards the concrete. It is not science that would establish us by itself on the level of the real, identified with what is positive, while metaphysics would distance us from it. Indeed, the object of science is itself only real and concrete through the presence of the universal that metaphysics considers. Science holds onto only certain aspects of being, because within this abstraction it can determine and fix them. But how would the real keep itself whole in what is thus delimited in a successive manner by the scientific understanding? This standpoint of understanding consists in leaving aside the very consideration of the being that we nevertheless assume as always given and underlying the determinations on which our observation is able to bear. But when we prolong the movement of our thought, we are seeking spontaneously to go beyond scientific abstraction, which focuses on the particular aspects of being and on the laws; we are seeking to grasp not a particular form of reality, but the meaning that the fact itself of being real should have in our eyes. However, if it is true that the natural movement of thought leads from scientific explication to metaphysical reflection, this entirely novel attitude will presuppose a quite manifest change of level. The universality considered by metaphysics is of an entirely different order than the partial abstractions of the sciences, it is that of a notion present in a varied way in the object of each of the positive sciences. Consequently, the consideration of universal being is not exactly of the same nature as that of each of the particular aspects of the real. From this, it seems to us, comes that secret resistance that thought sometimes feels when it wants truly to situate itself on the level of metaphysical reflection. To accede to it, it is not enough to add the results of the positive sciences to one another; it is necessary somehow to pass on to the limit, to grasp the direct relation that unites the singular to universal being and to comprehend that one does not pass from one to the other by the series of determinations that are the exclusive object of the [scientific] understanding. And yet it is to this final point that thought is led when it adopts an attitude of fidelity. We raise ourselves to the metaphysical level when we do not refuse to think expressly what the condition is thanks to which we think all the rest.

However, it is one thing to think somehow according to *the metaphysical dimension*,[3] another thing to arrive at a metaphysical explication in its rigor. Driven by the spontaneous movement of our thought, we would like to recognize the real in its universality, as well as in the intimacy of its perfections. But the truth is that the progression that leads us from the determinations of the understanding to the recognition of the universal presence of being precludes us from being able to exhaust our intellectual knowledge of it. It is doubtless quite easy, certainly, to rid ourselves of a rather too simple pretention to intellectual knowledge of the depth of things. How could thought come to grasp in a singular act, alongside the other aspects of the real, that very one that makes these abstractions possible? In particular, existence is never a determination like the others; to say it is in

3. Italics in the original. Throughout what follows, unless otherwise noted, the italics in the text are Forest's own.

relation to them like a beyond is precisely to say that at the moment where the understanding would succeed in presenting it [existence] to itself, fixing it in a representation, it would no longer be different from any one of the elements of abstract analysis that are its [the understanding's] proper object. Existence is never grasped in the same way as the ensemble of characteristics and laws that, on the contrary, always assume it. But since it is their foundation, it is impossible to get to the concrete without coming to dominate it in itself, if we can say so, to comprehend it along with the entire nature of the real. If this is the case, metaphysical thought, in its orientation to concrete reality, to the reality that is only such through the presence in it of universal being, would fail to grasp, to possess in an intellectual act, what is nonetheless the goal of its longing.

But actually, these remarks will allow us rather to discern, alongside purely illusory positions, the more precise meaning of what metaphysical explication ought to be. Metaphysics is not, properly speaking, the science of the concrete, rather it is, in opposition to phenomenalism, the intellectual vision capable of guaranteeing and establishing the reality of concrete perfections. Really situating itself on the level of concrete existence, it thus sets out to grasp its principle. So we will say that the metaphysical problem poses itself to us essentially under the form of a critical problem, in the sense that the original approach of thought consists in climbing back up from a given to the conditions that render it possible. Here is the real in the diversity of its aspects and the intimacy of its perfections. Doubtless it is given before any consideration of philosophic thought, it is given, for example, for a purely spontaneous and sensible knowing. But I know nothing as yet of the principles according to which it is given and that constitute it in its reality. I must thus in some way make it so that in critical reflection the world becomes real for me, passes in some way from an existence of fact to an existence of right, when I know myself capable of affirming being not only as given, but as connected to that alone which appears to me essential and primary. Original existence is somehow the departure point of my thought and the criterion of the value of its constructions. We could say, in this sense, that the metaphysical problem amounts to asking how we can be assured that the world given to us before metaphysical reflection as a fact, which we don't yet connect to its principle, exists also by right, exists truly. It is thus not a matter of transforming into an intellectual representation what doubtless surpasses all the determinations of the understanding; rather, it is a matter of grasping the principle of it, uncovering the foundations capable of bearing the universality of being and at the same time the diversity of singular perfections in which it comes to express itself. Doubtless metaphysics assumes at its starting point a kind of submission, a docility at once to the real and to the nature itself of thought, but it doesn't define itself solely by this. Let us say that if metaphysical thought assumes an attitude of *fidelity*, the metaphysical explication is an effort of *conquest*.

It seems to us that if one holds to these indications, which remain, one sees, provisory and incomplete, there would not be any essential difference between the diverse attitudes of metaphysical thought. In particular, the position itself of the metaphysical problem doesn't appear different according to idealism, at least in its absolute form, and to what we will call in a general way the ontological attitude, but what permits the setting of these doctrines into opposition, we are going to see, is the consideration of the method by which one or the other sets out to attain their essential goal. Reflection always feels itself, in effect, arrested and incomplete when it focuses on particular aspects of the real, it knows there is a beyond that escapes it and that it wants to attain. It is this movement that the aspiration of idealist philosophies for the concrete conveys; they are only an effort to go beyond the determinations we would take for the real itself, beyond what isolates and arrests the movement of thought. The ontological attitude also assumes from its starting point the same opposition between the abstractions of science and the formal object it sets out to consider, the being taken in all its universality, in which are immanent the particular objects of the scientific understanding. It is therefore in both cases the same reality to be attained, and metaphysical reflection always proceeds from the consideration of what might arrest it, it is an effort to go past these limits, to deliver itself from this sort of original gravity that fixes us in abstract determinations. We could indeed, without artifice, connect the problem of determination to that of abstraction, if by this latter term we expressly mean the examination of the spirit that focuses on genera, which exclude one another, and precisely from which metaphysical thought delivers us when it takes for formal object the universality of being. We would therefore express the meaning of this movement of thought by saying that it always consists in leading us *beyond the abstract understanding.*

It is not enough, however, to discern the task metaphysical thought must undertake, it remains still to determine the method capable of leading us to the goal. There the opposition between idealism and the ontological attitude appears considerable and we propose to denote it as one between *conversion* and *consent.* Since it is a matter of going beyond the determinations of the understanding, one could assume, first, that thought will find within itself, in the experience of connection and synthesis, that type of reality that escapes determinations, and that would be able consequently to serve as the foundation of phenomena, giving them in some way the being they don't have in themselves, the being that the objective vision can't enable us to grasp. Metaphysics would thus presuppose a kind of provisory refusal of objective being, but through the conversion of thought to its own interiority, it would find itself in the final analysis closer to the principles it is a question of reaching. The true nature of existence could therefore not be grasped for thought from the viewpoint of objectivity. We can, however, understand this same necessity for a deepening of the objective givens[4] according to a quite different attitude, one that we will call the attitude of consent to being. This is because objective thought doesn't always place itself on the level itself of the universality of being; we confine ourselves ordinarily to the object of a consideration fixed in an act of partial abstraction. Perhaps, however, it would suffice, in order to be led to the metaphysical principle, to accept truly thinking along the line of universality, or what comes to the same thing, on the level of the concrete; it would suffice to renounce that arresting of thought which only comes from ourselves, from our hesitation to go beyond the

4. Forest's term *données* might also be translated as "data," and elsewhere in the book, his *donnée* as "datum." I have chosen throughout to render the French as "givens" and "given," sticking closely to the literal Latin meaning, partly because the sense of "gift" seems especially appropriate in light of the explication of being that Forest is developing, and partly also because in current popular usage, "data" tends to be more narrowly associated with computer technology.

object of scientific understanding. It is easy to see there is an analogy between these two methods; in both cases, it is a matter of going beyond an incomplete vision, the imperfection of which has the same origin, that of determination and isolation. The attempt has often been made to convey this new orientation from which metaphysics sprang. Such is, for example, the meaning of the oppositions often noted between the concept and the idea, or in another way, between the concept and the judgment, the phenomenon and being, determinations and existence, analysis and synthesis. These oppositions that modern philosophy doesn't cease to consider go back to the distinction established by Kant between the understanding and reason. The doctrine of consent to being retains something of this, perhaps even the essential, as much as the idealist conversion, because in both cases it is a matter of winning through to a certain representation of the real beyond its determinations, a matter in sum, following Boutroux's expression, of discerning, for the sake of combatting in our consciousness, "the original intervention of the understanding which instead of limiting itself to studying reality lends it a form adapted to its own tendencies."[5] However, the two doctrines we are proposing to consider don't come together in this refusal alone, they join each other again in what they contain of the positive. Indeed, thought could not reach the metaphysical principles if, in returning to itself, it did not grasp in some way an impulse within that leads it beyond. The conversion understood in this way assumes, then, a form of consent; this is the consent that thought gives to itself, to its proper nature, when it somehow agrees to make good use of itself, and thus to justify concrete existence while avoiding skepticism. By the same token, in the ontological attitude we will go to the principle of the real by this alone, that we consent to think according to all its characteristics, all its essential implications, the object on which our thought focuses when we take it in all its universality. The consent of thought to being would then be not only the movement that establishes it on the metaphysical level, but also the method that allows it to climb up to the principle of concrete existence. Therefore, in both cases, metaphysics would presuppose an orientation and a method

5. Forest does not provide a citation for this quotation. Please see the "Note about Notes" in the translator's introduction concerning the scarcity of footnotes in Forest's original text.

analogous in their diversity, the consent of thought to itself or the consent of thought to being.

The essay we propose to undertake will therefore focus on the method of metaphysics. But if the two doctrines on which we would like to reflect entail a certain analogy in their development, their initial reasoning or, if you wish, their *fieri*,[6] this similarity will again be noted, with the same characteristics, in the conclusions at which they arrive. We would thus like, after having tried to determine which is the more rigorous method, to try to clarify the metaphysical meaning of existence by making use of interpretations of the two doctrines that shed light on one another. The metaphysical conclusions would thereby appear in a more rigorous way if they were attached to one problem alone, which is, in fact, that of the nature of abstraction. On the other hand, those problems that metaphysics encounters would be posed without any artifice, it seems to us, if we succeeded in showing how they arise from this alone, that thought renounces the limiting of its own movement. To try to follow something like the genesis of metaphysical thought is at the same time to discern the meaning of the problems it will have to resolve. They are somehow implied in that will to lead explication beyond abstract determinations, but it remains to try to find under what condition abstractions focusing only on genera and laws will truly be surpassed, under what condition we will rediscover concrete reality in all its actuality. It remains to ensure the rectitude of the movement that renders thought always more receptive to being, matching the amplitude of its claims to the universality of the object on which it is focusing.

6. "becoming"

2

The Idealist Conversion

When thought is faithful to its essential orientation, it is carried by its spontaneous movement towards objective being. But the spirit will not fix itself in this contemplation, and as if in this possession, without trying to justify in some way that very thing that is given to us, by raising itself to the recognition of the principles on which it depends. Now is it certain that objective thought has in itself the resources capable of taking us there? Idealism is first of all an attitude of defiance towards this move in our thought. Our preceding analyses can help us comprehend the origin of this defiance. Objective thought risks being for us only what fixes itself in the determinations of the understanding, which it would take for the real itself, and philosophy ought to have as its goal taking us beyond this imperfect intellection. The history of ideas, in particular the history of medieval doctrines, demonstrates that the danger is far from illusory. Thought does not renounce the tendency that carries it towards the real, but carried by that same instinct it slips into insoluble difficulties when it sees being only from the point of view of a realism of the understanding. These are difficulties of the same kind that reappear in modern philosophy when the understanding wants to impose on the real the form of its own tendencies. So we comprehend how intellectual thought, thus understood, far from placing us in the presence of being, would make us sort of slide along the surface of the real, keeping us only on the level of abstract determinations. For all the more reason objective thought will not enable us to grasp the principles of being if it fixes itself in the partial abstractions wherein it finds no impulse for going further. A philosophy oriented towards the concrete will therefore set out to avoid those dangers that not only scientific phenomenalism but often also certain philosophies of inferior realism bring in their wake. So let us not say in an immediate, uncritical way that we should turn away from the directions of objective thought. It is still necessary to recognize the necessity of a progression, of a deepening, of a passage from one genus to another, whether along the line of objective thought, or through an inversion of the habitual course of thought. It is within this orientation that we will be able to discern the principles of a philosophy of the concrete.

Idealism is the doctrine that demands from us a conversion when we set out to resolve the problem of being. It asks us to mistrust objective thought, to come back from the consideration of the object to that of the interior act from which it proceeds and that constitutes it. But this conversion indicates, inversely, a trust in the value of thought, in the resources at its disposal for discerning the nature of an absolute foundation. It's not possible, according to idealism, that thought keep only to what is formal in being, and that it be condemned to leaving out of its grasp some principle of the real it cannot itself comprehend, but is obliged only to note without mastering. Idealism is, thus understood, an orientation towards the concrete. So we go on to ask ourselves if the method it adopts allows it to attain the level of singular existence, or if, on the contrary, it is not condemned precisely by this method to remain before an abstract it takes for the real itself.

It's quite a natural attitude, it seems to us, that we adopt in seeking to clarify the exact meaning of the metaphysical method, by reflecting on the nature of the obstacles that prevent thought from advancing. The reflection of idealism will focus in the first place, then, on the origin of the difficulties it must overcome. Now we know that the method we should follow is that which will finally assure our victory over what remains inadequate in the reasonings of the abstract understanding. So let us try to better grasp the nature of the illusions of the understanding that distance us from being; in doing so we will doubtless better see the method that will open up access to it for us. The real, we say, is always something other than the indefinitely expanded sum of abstract notions; but this remark doesn't by itself take us forward enough in the metaphysical analysis. That the real is not abstract, this does not at all imply that abstraction is not a legitimate process of thought; so it remains to look in a more precise way for what the deformation of the understanding consists in and how we can avoid it. Now doesn't it appear that to the method of abstraction and analysis is joined, in a quite constant way, maybe without our knowing it, another attitude, that of isolation? Indeed, let us follow the habitual movement of conceptual thought. The process it adopts is that of seeking the simple; in the presence of the rich diversity of things and the variety of their aspects, it tries, in order to comprehend them, to discover the elements that can be discerned in them. However, the abstract givens, which are only obtained by the movement of regressive thought, and which thus take their meaning according to the primitive synthesis from which thought has its starting point, soon risk being abandoned at the end of this development, and so sliding into the fixity, the immobility of the thing. We forget the meaning they have in the true act of thought and the relative character we ought to maintain for them. Thus it is true that concrete being can be grasped under the aspect of number, space, and motion, but will we make these elements towards which conceptual thought raises itself the starting points for a construction that would claim to grasp realities? We certainly see the danger of this proceeding. To realize is always to fix, to determine, and then to isolate; so it all happens as if thought, encountering in its progress notions that only have meaning within this interior activity, and under the relative aspect it maintains for them, were to abandon them, so to speak, leaving them behind like things, while pushing the movement of analysis further. We end up then with a vision one could call realist, since the results of the thought-activity are fixed in themselves, but it appears in a manifest enough way that this vision fails to help us grasp the real in its plenitude. The abstractions of the understanding are taken, then, strictly speaking, as things; we no longer comprehend them as relative to a beyond that they designate in a virtual way, without permitting us to represent expressly to ourselves all that they imply. The elements isolated by the effort of reduction and analysis are distanced from veritable reality because they lack foundation, they are detached at the same time as abstract, and the act of thought that would fix them in themselves thereby makes them lose even the provisory, incomplete, and relative reality belonging to the abstract. Hence the danger of a thought that wants to stick to the determinations is that it soon risks having no more than realized abstractions.

This being the case, what is the spiritual activity that would allow us to rediscover the concrete? Wouldn't it be not what takes us into the presence of the elements but into the actual experience of the connection whereby they are assembled? If the possible error for the understanding is before all that of isolation and abstraction being taken for the real itself, metaphysical thought will fulfill its work by being aware of the true conditions of the synthetic connection. This is essentially the attitude that idealism proposes we adopt by first recognizing the exceptional importance of the truth delivered to us in the Spinozist formula: *omnis determinatio negatio.*[1] To assure the reality of being is first to grasp the true nature of an activity of reference and of connection. Now, it is the essential task of idealism to avoid the abstract by placing itself at a viewpoint where nothing is isolated, where everything, on the contrary, communicates and affirms itself as real. Indeed, let us assume that we have been able to grasp, beyond the results of analysis, the true nature of this synthetic activity. We would be able to say, then, that we have truly discerned the principle of being, since it is this foundation alone that gives the elements their reality, and that in their isolation they are cut off, so to speak, from being. In the truth of the synthesis, on the contrary, the form of everything, by dominating the distinction of the parts, gives them, properly speaking, their being, and not only their intelligibility. Thus understood, idealism sets out only to find the principles of the real; it is one of the possible responses to the problem posed by metaphysical thought when it is faithful to the spontaneous movement that raises it beyond scientific explication.

1. "all determination is negation."

However, according to this doctrine, the reality of the synthetic act could not be apparent to us when we focus ourselves on things; it could not be given at all by the realism of the understanding. Entirely to the contrary, comprehending that the reality of being is only possible through synthesis, idealism demands from us a conversion by which we would return from the given to the consciousness, from the object to the act, to interiority. If objective representation fails to place us in the presence of being, if ignoring the synthetic perspective makes us sort of glide along the surface of things, while rendering us incapable of penetrating them, then we must so to speak reverse the movement of thought that, far from carrying us towards the real, keeps us instead at a distance. Consequently, reflection is the only method that will help us to grasp the reality of thought at the same time as its object. The subject grasps itself, then, in its purely spiritual activity, it appears to us as interiority, and not as one thing among other things. Indeed, alongside the represented elements there must be an act that is subject for itself, and no more simply an object for others. It is by placing itself in this perspective that thought grasps itself in its act of reference and connection; from then on it no longer risks missing the reality of being, since the synthesis alone is capable of constituting its foundation. But if the reality of being is given with that of the synthesis, there must be, in order to grasp its principle, a conversion by which we come back to ourselves, and as it were a kind of provisory refusal of being, which will allow us finally better to possess it by dominating it. The method of metaphysics is therefore this return by which thought comes back to itself, seems in this way to forget the real, but moves away from it in order better to find its principle within itself. Seeking to become truly interior to itself, the subject is not by this exterior to other things; it is only, through reflection, setting aside the abstract symbols that come between the real and ourselves. The movement of thought we have just sketched out is that which the most important of contemporary idealist philosophies propose to follow. It is this effort that appears to us to constitute them distinctively, when, after numerous analyses but with some distance, we try to discern their essential movement. Philosophy is not satisfied with insisting on the perfection of a concrete world; it wants to climb up to the affirmation of the principle on which its being depends; it wants finally this discernment of the principle to be grasped in the very effort through which thought orients itself towards the concrete. Philosophy wants the method for attaining the real in an absolute way, that is, in a vision that leaves nothing outside it, to be given solely in the consideration of the object it is examining. Now, if the object appropriate to metaphysical thought is the concrete, it will be enough to justify it in a definitive way by reflecting on the reasons for metaphysical thought being prevented from reaching it, then substituting for these methods the one that would be better adapted. And if the conversion to interiority helps us to grasp the reality of the synthetic act, which constitutes the real itself, we must say, in fact, that the principle of the method and the principle of metaphysics only go to make one. But actually, the functions of the spirit that we bring into play in this metaphysical determination are quite different. They have this in common, that they entail the truth of connection, of a dynamic development, and that they always take into account those somehow practical and moral elements the idealist synthesis implies. Because these doctrines intend to find in the spiritual activity itself the conditions that permit the affirmation of the reality of metaphysical being, we are first going to follow up the experience they constitute, and if the idealist conversion doesn't appear capable of effectively taking us beyond the abstract, we will try to discern another method better adapted to that end.

The Philosophy of Judgment

The idealist conversion is the movement that brings us back from consideration of the object to the experience of the interior act that allows us to affirm its truth or reality. Now this opposition, in its simplest and most general form, can present itself to us as that between the concept and the judgment; understood in this way, it could then provide for metaphysical reflection its immediate starting point. Philosophy would thus propose to get to being, to the concrete, through this inversion of the habitual direction of thought, [an inversion] that would have us grasp not the object of the judgment, considered as a thing, but the activity itself that constitutes it. This attitude, we see, makes use of what is perhaps essential in the Bergsonian philosophy; it is the starting point of a doctrine of capital importance for our current sketch, that of Mr. Brunschvicq, the main lines of which we first want to indicate, underscoring the interest it has in our eyes, even though we are seeking to submit it to critical examination.

The essential goal of Brunschvicq's philosophy is to "disengage the notion of the pure subject from any representational element," and thus to avoid subordinating the freedom of the knowing subject to a representation or a concept of the object. Thus understood, it is therefore the outcome of the reflexive method inherited from Maine de Biran and reprised above all by Jules Lagneau. It intends above all to ensure the originality of interior being, to avoid drawing consciousness back to the objective nature of the substance or the thing. But what particularly interests us is seeing how Brunschvicq wants to ensure, in this attitude, the reality that common sense, science, and philosophy itself recognize in the thought object. And first, can we say that thought is capable of certifying truly what is, in affirming its objective reality? Doubtless the judgment of reality depends on what we can call "the form of exteriority," of the shock received by the spirit when in relationship with a foreign reality. But this pure shock, the condition of thought, is indeterminate, ungraspable in itself, it can't guarantee the reality of existence. Thus it is that the sensation can be given without the affirmation of existence, for example, in the case of hysterics, and inversely, the image can acquire, in a hallucination under hypnosis, the consistency of the thought object. In order for the object of the affirmation to become reality, the fact must be incorporated into the general system of the consciousness; thought defines itself then through "the form of interiority." It is itself, therefore, the function that posits being, and "for critical reflection the world can be only in the spirit, it is the spirit that makes it exterior to itself, that extends to the entire universe it comprehends in this universal judgment, the primitive exteriority of 'that is.'"[2] Consequently, there is no more posing of the problem of the nature of being independently of the act through which it is affirmed, since it finds itself entirely constituted by it. "In a word, the nature of being hangs on the nature of the affirmation of being."[3]

2. Léon Brunschvicq, *La modalité du jugement* (coll. "Bibliothèque de la philosophie contemporaine"; Paris: Alcan, 1897), 134. [Forest's own citation]

3. Brunschvicq, *La modalité du jugement*, 78. [Forest's own citation]

Therefore, at the starting point of philosophical reflection, we must dismiss the fundamental principle of realism, which consists in representing being as a given.[4] It is this same development that will permit us to comprehend the effective conditions of scientific knowledge. From the perspective of the scientific understanding, the given would be the concept, and yet modern science begins only at the moment Descartes liberates the intelligence from the yoke of the concept. To comprehend is not to classify, it is to measure, and better yet, to connect; it is to establish the relations that give their meaning to the terms and from which, properly speaking, one can say they themselves proceed. Such is the guiding idea by which Brunschvicq organizes his slow and subtle analyses of the progress of mathematics and of the constitution of physical causality in human experience. But conceptual thought doesn't succeed only in arresting the spontaneous movement of scientific thought; indeed, it's the same deformation we find again in the abstract constructions of conceptual ontology, as it appears in Hegel or in Hamelin. These doctrines try to fix in the form of thesis or antithesis and to express in a concept everything produced in time, including the law itself of the progression of the real. But to what realities can such abstractions correspond? These are, one could say, possible realities that precede actual existence. But doesn't it seem that we find here, in the most manifest way, the error of the understanding that realizes its object independently of the movement in which it should be integrated and makes of it a reality in itself? Such is the nature, absolutely illusory, of the possible, because what would only be possible, inasmuch as it is distinguished from the real, is exactly equivalent to the impossible. Therefore, let us not try to place ourselves before the objective givens imagined, even under the name of relation, by the conceptualism of Hamelin, following that of Hegel. It is all too clear that by this method we will never attain the real, and it is the case that through a quite singular error, the most certain way to distance ourselves from metaphysical being is to try to make of every affirmation the representation of a given.

According to Brunschvicq, we will get to the final reason for all these failures by reflecting anew on the most important characteristic of all abstract representation. The philosophical problem to which all

4. See translator's note 4 on p. 13.

these reasonings of thought bring us back could be posed in these terms: Is determination the condition of being? Now, we know that determination is the principal characteristic of the concept. Therefore, the understanding's representation is going to assimilate all that is determined to an object in space. The object of thought will thus take on the character of being, but first will only be an abstraction, then will be isolated because, according to the dilemma that makes for the profound significance of the *Parmenides*: being is the negation of the one, the one is the negation of being.[5] There is thus only one way to ensure the philosophical reality of being, which is to realize in ourselves the conversion that authentic idealism demands of us. It is to forget entirely all objective representation, to comprehend that true intelligence has nothing in common with conceptual thought. The representation from which the realist imagination proceeds, closely followed by the imagining of transcendence, doesn't even correspond to the position of the being that it isolates and that it destroys in this isolation. The real is nowhere else than in the progression of thought, it is this movement itself, when we deliver it from all that conceptual ontology still allowed to subsist in it of the unreal and the abstract. If Renan could say that "humanity makes the sanctity of what it believes and the beauty of what it loves," we can say, according to the same inspiration, that the real is entirely determined in the purely immanent, autonomous constructions of intellectual activity. This is because all other vision, far from putting us before the real, pushes us away and leaves it distanced. Will one say that intellectual activity is itself subject to determination and thus pushes us away from the real? But all to the contrary, the principle of determination does not apply to the nature of the spirit, which, never being an object even for itself, does not therefore at any moment lack reality:

> Thought is an infinite faculty of unification, it is a radical spontaneity, from which it is necessary to conclude that to make thought into an object of reflection, even for itself, is to distance it from the reality of the spontaneity in which it appears. Being cannot become an object of thought, were it only separated through abstraction from what is the subject itself of thought, or expressed

5. See Plato, *Parmenides* 141e, for the posing of this dilemma.

> in terms of an object, because in every object, as Leibniz notes, there is extension. The idealism positing being as a function of thought conceives it on the type of that radical spontaneity we have attempted to define.[6]

Brunschvicq's philosophy thus really takes on the character of a doctrine that, in the continuous tradition of idealism, is everywhere in pursuit of the concrete. It is clear that in the end it recognizes itself as removed from all abstraction. It is the prolongation of the Cartesian science that conceives of no other reality than singular; it dismisses from metaphysical reflection all questions where the imagining of the possible and the abstract could reappear. Thought stands before the real world that it constitutes itself, it wouldn't know how to interrogate itself at the same time about the given and its own genesis, making itself somehow at once younger and older than it is.[7] It is enough to have really understood the nature of the realist imagination in order to grasp the illusory character of those questions in which Brunschvicq sees, strictly speaking, only a residue of abstraction.

Now let us try to lay out before us in as clear and objective way as possible the nature of the movement of thought we have just followed. The critique of philosophical doctrines doubtless does not consist in seizing in them some insufficiency in the progression they want to accomplish, but, so to speak, in exiting this movement itself in order better to see the goal to which it tends and the character of truth it might have in its spontaneity. Here before our eyes is the vision that the scientific understanding, soon followed by the realist imagination, offers us. It is only abstraction, and consequently, insufficiency. It is thus natural to think of grasping the real there, where nothing is abstract or isolated, and consequently identifying the real with the movement by which thought constitutes its object in the autonomy of its act. So we must say that there is nothing beyond freedom, that thought goes beyond its object, in the same way as love, when it is not a requirement but a gift, and that at last philosophy completes itself when we have been raised up to recognize in ourselves "a principle of

6. Brunschvicq, *L'idéalisme contemporain* (coll. "Bibliothèque de la philosophie contemporaine"; Paris, Alcan, 1905), 79. [Forest's own citation]

7. See Plato, *Parmenides* 141c, d.

communion that the immanence of reason bars us from realizing or symbolizing independently of the act of communion itself."[8] It is clear, indeed, that this act will not entail the character of insufficiency we have had to recognize in the object of representation. But it remains to know whether it will help us to grasp the real itself, and whether in a certain way the rigor of the movement of thought doesn't leave us in the presence of a new abstraction. Doubtless it is indispensable that the aspects of the real not be isolated but connected. Is this to say that we should for all that identify the real with the act itself of connection? This act must still bear, by its very spontaneity, not only on the form of truth or intelligibility, but also on actual existence. Now this is a problem that certain forms of idealism engage, but that Brunschvicq refuses to pose. The spirit, he says, answers only for itself, for the intelligible and the true, not for the existence of nature. This amounts to saying that thought only exerts itself in its creations by assuming a given it doesn't any longer construct but receives. Now, it is certainly possible that we possess no resource for pushing analysis to this final point, in order to assume nothing and leave nothing outside our consideration. But if scientific thought is able to make progress with this attitude, nonetheless we will not say that metaphysical reflection has reached the goal it intended. Indeed, it couldn't transform the hope of success into a positive gain and, attesting that the error of abstract representation lies in isolation, identify concrete reality with the progression of the judgment, if we didn't still show how this progression allows us to determine and clarify through the principles of metaphysical thought even the principles that render possible the constitution of the positive sciences—that is, the contingency of concrete being. A doctrine that would halt itself before a given, without grasping in the act of judgment some intuitive force for going beyond it, would appear to us still as a philosophy of the abstract. This is why we should examine whether, despite first appearances, the doctrines of objective idealism wouldn't comprise, better than the philosophy of judgment, the rigorous character of a doctrine of the concrete.

8. Brunschvicq, *Le progrès de la conscience dans la philosophie occidentale* (coll. "Bibliothèque de la philosophie contemporaine"; Paris: Alcan, 1927), 791. [Forest's own citation]

The Synthetic Method

The essential character of idealism should be sought not in the affirmations this doctrine eventually permits, but rather in the method that renders them possible, in the movement of thought from which they can never be separated. Idealism sets out only to make manifest the philosophical exigency of the reflective method, and the insufficiency of the perspective of objective representation, incapable of helping us grasp the reality of being and of thought. Indeed, if the method of the understanding is that of isolation and abstraction, one comprehends how the interior act of thought operates conciliation, puts us back in the presence of the unity, and at the same time the intelligibility, of being, of its truth. Only it is still of a somewhat formal character; determining the conditions that make it so that the real is given for science, the philosophy of judgment does not purport to end in any interpretation valid for the absolute of the real. However, idealism cannot keep itself within these limits; in bringing being back to thought, it must strive to dismiss everything that separates one from the other, so that the movement of thought will still be the ideal genesis of the real. This doctrine is not a refusal to pose the problem of being, but the affirmation that thought alone is capable of providing us with the principle of true existence. This would be, we see, the true way of dismissing phenomenalism, to take into account all that the analysis of being assumes, because its constitution is identified with the purely autonomous act of thought, and by this to realize the ambition of a philosophy that wants to go beyond all determination. Now, how could these results be achieved? If idealism is only the return of thought onto itself in the determination of principles, it must therefore be that a deepening of this method would lead us further than the results already obtained by the philosophy of judgment. The reflective analysis must reach, through the deepening of the consciousness itself, the point where the interiority of the spirit permits comprehension of the reality of objective being and the complete immanence of being to thought. Everything happens therefore as though, in the first doctrine we have just examined, the conversion that idealism demands were still incomplete and superficial, but it is the prolongation of the same movement towards interiority that should help us to recognize the metaphysical foundations of concrete being. This, it seems to us, is the spirit of the doctrines of French idealism whose principles we would like to examine, not in the historical order of appearance of the systems, but according to the progressive order of what appears to us to be, in its diverse manifestations, the idealist experience.

Reflection is the act by which thought separates from its objects or its material the form that it there applies and realizes. Therefore, when we attempt to be perfectly interior to ourselves, we are seeking first to turn away from all objective consideration, and what alone appears to us is the movement of thought applied to knowing the world, incapable of grasping itself in the pure state, but distinct for the transcendental analysis of the objects that it renders present by constituting their connection. It suffices, then, to push the analysis far enough so as to go beyond the empirical elements that one can discern in a positive way. Psychology leads from itself to metaphysics, or rather it is metaphysics, if we understand by that the affirmation of the super-sensible, of what is not given and realized on the level of phenomena, but which is nevertheless the condition that makes them possible. There is thus in the thinking subject an element of universality and of the absolute, which raises it beyond the determinable reality of what is outside it and even beyond the existence of phenomena. It is this transcendental reality, not empirical, that reflection has as its mission to grasp; in order to arrive there, it doubtless suffices to analyze in a philosophical way no matter what content of our consciousness. Let us suppose, then, that we grasp in ourselves, following that truly classic method of Kant, the transcendental act of judgment. Thus we are in the presence of a purely formal element, which the Kantian critique has never asked to justify the reality of its object on the level of being, or to allow us to reach the foundation on which the existence of phenomena rests. It therefore remains to understand how we could make use of a Kantian method for the solution of a problem that is not Kantian.

Let us start with the very obvious remark that thought grasps itself as act, not as object or essence. Now what is it that prevents us from getting to the real and from grasping the essential principle that ensures its existence? We were saying it is, before all, the habitual but perhaps artificial method of the analysis that isolates the elements it reaches from the act by which they have been grasped, and thus abandons them to the indeterminateness and the void of all abstraction. How would this method allow us to reach the absolute of being, or more simply, the real? The element, separated from the ensemble from which it is extracted, is incapable of subsisting by itself; therefore, at the same time that it is isolated, it lacks the character of substance, and this is doubtless the nature of the given when we consider it simply as the object of our thought, when we fix and determine it in this way, believing we are realizing it in itself, but on the contrary leaving it detached from its principles and foundations. We understand, therefore, how the act of thought can permit us to affirm being; by coming back to the act, which is no longer itself a purely subjective reality and of an empirical nature, we reach the principle on which we can have the existence of phenomena depend. It is no longer only the connection that would ensure the unity of the representation, but it is already the relation from which the elements derive their nature, their specific reality. The form of the whole thus constitutes not only the intelligibility of the elements but, properly speaking, their being. Such is, it seems to us, for one of its essential aspects, the inspiration of idealism. It's in the doctrine of Hamelin, we know, that we must look for its most clear-cut expression, when his *Essai* shows us not only that relation is one category among others, but more, that it is the method thanks to which we can construct all of them, including actual existence, which under the form of personality, is only the relation of self to self. In this system, relationship is really the simplest form of thought, which it cannot deny of itself when it affects to be brought back, below the richness of representation, to that element grasped in the simplest experience of the act of thought. In following these indications, then, we could understand how synthetic idealism wants us to grasp the principle that constitutes metaphysical being, through the simple deepening of reflection.

But in order to resolve this same problem, we can follow another direction, which we find indicated above all in Lachelier and in Lagneau, and which is assumed in the entire rhythm of thought of French idealism. Through reflection, we were saying, thought turns away from objective representation and focuses on its act itself, on which the reality distinct from it is going to depend. It is the nature of this passage that must be understood and that constitutes all the difficulty of the dialectic, of the synthesis. Now we know that thought does not grasp itself as a thing, it is never an object among other objects, and that same character that seems to raise it beyond reality and being is going to allow us to comprehend how, on the contrary, it can be their principle. What, indeed, is that reality known as what is never an object, what can't even fix itself in a given that would become the object of some observation? It's what we call not being but value; thus thought, in its form alone, in the act that for transcendental analysis is distinct from its objects, takes on in our eyes the reality of what ought to be, of what does not subsist as a done thing. Thought is not a fact, let us understand by this that its nature is not determinable from outside by a method that would proceed from known objects to the subject that thinks them, but let us also recognize that thought is value, that is to say consent, the interior freedom following which it is not satisfied to be itself, but accepts to use itself well; in this way, it wants itself and affirms itself in its absolute value. Now, if thought grasped first as an act of connection could appear to us already as the metaphysical foundation of phenomena, for all the more reason will we find in this idea of value and in that of the ideal the reason for the passage to objective being. There you have what Lachelier's dialectic seeks to bring to light, for when we look for what should support the truth of experience, we say first that it is, it has been, and it will be, and it is this last case, apparently the thorniest of the three, that gives us finally the key to the two others. To say that the truth will be is to say, in effect, that it ought to be, and that there is a reason that determines it to be, and that reason, founded on the affirmation of value and the ideal is what constitutes the true interior nature of thought. The doctrine is found perhaps more clearly yet in Jules Lagneau:

> When the value of the sensible world and the intelligible world dissipates, it's that the spirit doesn't comprehend that it has value only through its relation with what has none by itself, that the true value is beyond. There is the truly realist idealism. What makes the reality of what is is its relation with what is not, which excludes existence, but consists in the position itself of being and existence.[9]

9. Jules Lagneau, *De l'existence de Dieu*, (coll. "Bibliothèque de la philosophie contemporaine"; Paris: Alcan, 1925), 67. [Forest's own citation]

Reflection indeed finds the true foundation of the real in that character of thought that, raised beyond being, *consents to its own nature* and to that of all its objects. This philosophy of contingence, also manifest as much in Boutroux and Hamelin as in Lachelier and Lagneau, is found underlying all French idealism. Beyond the phenomena, which are only its manifestation, appears for refection the reality of the free act, according to which, finally, to be is to be willed, or put another way, to deserve to be, because it is the Good alone that bears in itself its reason. Now, the principle with which we reach the absolute of the real is indeed that which we can grasp in the return of thought to itself; analysis discerns it at the same time as it recognizes in thought a nature superior to that of phenomena, of represented objects or, if you wish, of things. The foundation of metaphysical being is found therefore in the pure intellectual subject, that is, "not in a particular type of representation, but in the act of giving an objective value to our sensible representations."[10]

We see, in this way, the nature of the connection between thought and being that is established. We had, at first sight, believed we grasped in reflection only the abstract form of thought. Idealism wants to show us it is nothing of the sort. First, if thought grasps itself as act, this act is precisely what phenomena were lacking to acquire the character of being; they subsist in effect, not in themselves, but in the absolute nature of thought. But one can go further in the affirmation of unity. Thought grasps itself in some way as the form or as the act that gives to experience all the substance of the real, indeed it finds in itself the absolute basis of this passage. At the same time as it is an act of connection, it is value and freedom; thus thought consents to the reality of the objects it opens itself to. It affirms its own value in accepting to seek itself outside [itself]. This is what Lachelier expresses in a bold metaphor:

> I agree quite willingly that we must not look for the spirit outside the facts it informs and in which it realizes itself. There is no more thinking substance than there is extended thought. I don't even think that it is necessary to speak of absolute subject or of universal thought, as

10. Jules Lachelier, *Psychologie et métaphysique* (coll. "Bibliothèque de la philosophie contemporaine", Paris: Alcan, 1924), 157. [Forest's own citation]

> if thought pre-existed things or could be something outside them. Thought is truth, and the truth is in the things themselves. It is there the spirit should seek itself if it wants to find itself, and we can say of it, according to the words of the Gospel, that it finds itself only in losing itself.[11]

In climbing up in this way to the idea of the Good, or rather in grasping this idea implied in the simplest act of thought, which is at once connection and value, idealism raises itself to an original and firm vision of the real. In a sort of metaphysical ascesis we appear first to pull away from the real, we focus our thought uniquely on the consideration of the synthesis that it itself is. But if we push the analysis far enough into the interior nature of the spirit, we are soon by that very reflection sent back to the real, we touch on the principle of its existence. Very far from being isolated and as if deprived of all solidity, the real is in and through this act of absolute thought which realizes itself in nature; following Boutroux's essential principle, "it is the act that explains the essence." As much as in the Aristotelian doctrine or even the Bergsonian, reality, from the idealist point of view, becomes that contingency that is underlaid by the reality of an act, the continuity of a progress or of a gift. But this absolute, immanent in phenomena, is the pure affirmation of their value, the positing of the universal and absolute of which they are then only the exterior manifestation. This vision of a philosophy of pure immanence is therefore what would offer us the highest perfection of the real, and philosophical thought doubtless leads us there above all by its care to avoid the illusions of the understanding, and to uncover, through the return to interiority, not only the abstract form of truth, but the foundation of being.

Idealism thus effectively ends in a doctrine of concrete being. The reality of nature is found, following the expression of Jules Lagneau, "welded to the absolute," thought and existence are posed in this way the one and the other, the one through the other, and it is through the reciprocity of this relation that they reach actual existence. Thought not only affirms itself, the synthetic act that it is

11. Lachelier, *Oeuvres*, tome II (coll. "Bibliothèque de la philosophie contemporaine"; Paris: Alcan, 1933), 126. [Forest's own citation]

for itself is also the true foundation of objective being; and when it consents to its own nature, it affirms and gives itself that of all its objects. But let's not simply consider the nature of this relation when it is fully constituted; it remains to know how it is realized and justified. It is on this problem of *the becoming of concepts* that, it seems to us, the essential remarks suggested by the idealist dialectic should focus.

The problem that is posed is really the one we have not ceased to consider, the problem of the relations between the abstract and the concrete or, put another way, between analysis and synthesis. Reflection is really an analysis that will allow us to grasp and in some measure isolate, in a transcendental way, the pure act of thought. But analysis is considered in such a way that it leads to synthesis, and it is on the nature of this passage that we should reflect. The same dialectic can be presented in somewhat different terms. The nature of thought, prior to the moment where it grasps itself in its objects, is always considered to be an incomplete and abstract reality, and we find very often in the doctrines of synthetic idealism terms that convey this provisory nature. Thus, the moral necessity that Lachelier has intervene is going to allow us to "pass beyond the sphere of abstraction and the void," it obliges thought to pass on from abstract existence, which is its proper form, to the existing subject, which gives to this form a content distinct from it. This character of an objective idealism is shown better still in Hamelin's doctrine:

> I have done much Greek philosophy, he writes, and a little bit of German. Now it seems to me that the Greeks and the Germans are not wrong to speculate boldly on concepts, or as Plato would say, on the ideas. The question of the reality of ideas should be posed anew in Kantianism itself, and it seems to me, it must be resolved affirmatively.[12]

It is from this essential character of a synthetic idealism that it gets caught up in the only difficulty we want to insist on. If idealism is a passage from the abstract to the concrete, it remains to find the reason that would allow justification of this passage in an absolute way.

12. Letter of July 18, 1887 to Mlle P., cited by René Le Senne, *Le Devoir*, (coll. "Bibliothèque de la philosophie contemporaine"; Paris, Alcan, 1930), 872. [Forest's own citation]

One would obviously not find in the synthesis, when it is achieved, the basis of the progress by which thought is raised to up to it. The strongest criticism against idealism would consist in saying that the only necessity we would be able to reach is the necessity that the real be; the synthesis would only succeed because we know that it must go to the being first given, to the reality the analysis of which could have first extricated the elements that would allow it to constitute itself. It is obviously necessary to find a basis for the passage from the abstract to the concrete and not to be satisfied with considering it as a fact. If it were a matter simply of affirming that the real is a whole, idealism would doubtless allow us to justify that conclusion, but it is necessary in a more profound way to see the universe *as a whole*, that is, to determine the principle upon which the necessity leading it to realize itself will depend. But as far as the idealist analysis pushes its effort of reduction, it will only find the elements with which the whole realizes itself, not the principle that actually ensures the connection, that possesses a metaphysical value sufficient in order to produce it. Indeed, how could one find in the insufficiency alone of the abstract the basis for passing to the concrete? The abstraction from which one starts is certainly anterior to the universality of being, because it is that of an incomplete element, the pure affirmation of truth, independently of the existing subject in which it realizes itself. Now, from the abstract thus understood, one can never derive anything, just as from the abstract notion of animality I will never derive that of rationality; it is necessary that the latter be added to it in an extrinsic way. This objection does not present merely a theoretical significance foreign to the logic itself of the system. It seems idealism would recognize something of its value, since it seeks to ensure the passage from the abstract to the concrete through a recourse that comes to add itself in some way to the original consideration of the abstract. In effect, if the necessity of this progression isn't of a purely logical and rational nature, we could yet consider a sort of moral necessity, that which determines the best to be. Doubtless metaphysical reflection attains by this a final foundation, but by having it intervene doesn't one exit a purely idealist philosophy, especially in its notional form? On the other hand, this intervention of a moral necessity in the dialectic will not permit avoiding the essential difficulty we want to consider in the relationship of the abstract to the concrete. How would a still abstract and unreal thought give to phenomena the being they don't have by themselves, the being that for its own part thought can only acquire through them? How would one have existence rest on this relationship between an original element having only the incompleteness of the abstract and an end-point still lacking the true firmness of the real?

Synthetic idealism therefore encounters one sole difficulty, but in our eyes an essential one, that which proceeds from *the priority of the abstract over the concrete.* The distinctive feature of these abstractions anterior to the universality of being, abstractions that idealism considers when it wants to construct being as the end-point of a development, is that nothing can be added from outside to what they define and fix. Metaphysical thought must therefore avoid either starting with abstraction, thus understood, or even passing through it. It would risk always finding itself trapped. The traveler who ventures onto the coastal sands instead of following the firm route will soon not be able to either advance farther or retreat, and every effort he makes to progress only makes the predicament worse. Thus, when thought lets itself be seduced by the incomplete, by an abstraction that would not at first signify the whole real and would not have to progress towards it, it can't return any longer to that concrete that it originally possessed, if not by right, at least in fact; much less will it be able to raise itself to the absolute. It remains caught in the indeterminate. Starting from an abstract law, we will ever obtain only a reality that conserves the same character, and it is not enough, it seems to us, to substitute for the determinations and analyses of the understanding the experience of the synthesis in order actually to get to being. The abstract form of the whole does not suffice to give by itself alone the being from which doubtless the elements, the terms of the analysis, the concepts have been stripped away.

The priority of the abstract over the concrete in the doctrines we have just examined was the foundation that seemed to allow in the most solid way realization of the ambition of idealism by ensuring the identity of being and thought. The one could not be without the other, in such a way that this philosophy of immanence led to a metaphysical view the rigor and simplicity of which we still want to emphasize. The ambition of metaphysics seemed very close to being achieved, thought riveted to being by composing at the same time as its nature its foundation, and if you wish, its substance. Idealism, thus understood, would really be realism itself, since the explication does not skim the surface of things but is identified with the absolute nature of its object. The interest of synthetic idealism is in its being that metaphysical construction where the perspectives of reflection and objectivism are united with the greatest originality. But don't the very rigor and simplicity of this construction in fact explain its final failure, and aren't they, in a certain manner, characteristics of pure abstraction? To pass from thought to being in a purely immanent way is to risk finally remaining on the level of that reality that one first recognizes as incomplete, incapable of being sufficient unto itself. The dialectic that wishes solidly to ensure the reality of experience in its relation to the absolute, according to the type of a purely immanent causality, would finally make us miss the reality of one as much as the other. But the world is present and actual, it defies all the vanity of our constructions; in that immediate presence that we cannot deny, but of which we only want to find the true principle, it is itself the guarantee of the worth of our systems. The failure of the idealist attempts would lead us then, at least in a negative and as if hypothetical way, to the conclusion that the real, whose absolute foundation we are seeking, only finds its solidity if it remains distinct from this very absolute. The connection that unites them must be thought in a more supple fashion than in the doctrines that look to realize unity in essence. Everything takes place as though the perfection of relation, according to the spirit of idealism, prevented the terms from acquiring the actual reality it ought to give them. But in whatever way we might represent its nature to ourselves, it is certainly in the relation that the terms are realized, that being itself is given, and if a philosophy of the concrete comes to be constituted, it will not be by forgetting this essential principle of idealism, but by seeking which inspiration would allow a construction to succeed, for which those of synthetic idealism would be like the image and analogue. In very great measure it is the metaphysical truth of concrete being that the nature of relation expresses; the position of being in existence cannot make us forget that it only is, in what constitutes it uniquely, through the metaphysical principle that goes beyond it. We must therefore only seek a way of getting away from abstraction by at the same time in some way making being relative and relation itself concrete.

3

Consent to Being

METAPHYSICAL THOUGHT CANNOT ADOPT a method other than that which allows it to pass beyond the consideration of isolated elements and in this way to achieve a spiritual possession of being through the discernment of the principles capable of justifying its universality, in the diversity of its concrete perfections. But if the idealist reflection fails to give us, along with the reality of the synthesis, that of the elements themselves, which it would identify with the form of the whole, it remains the case that thought might raise itself through an inverse method to a synthetic vision of the real. The natural movement of thought is not the act by which it comes back onto itself and turns away from the consideration of objective being. That being the case, why wouldn't we seek to follow its spontaneous approaches by prolonging them according to their essential orientation? Perhaps we must think that the difficulties encountered by thought in the completion of its metaphysical task come only from itself and, so to speak, from the insufficiency of its effort, from the arrest of its impulse. This is because if the concrete alone is real, it is always distant in some respect, so thought is going to stop at the simple determinations it can grasp. There is thus perhaps something like a hesitation in us to think on the level of concrete reality, to let ourselves be carried by the affirmation itself of the real to metaphysical horizons we don't want to contemplate. We fear letting ourselves be pulled beyond what we can grasp in the instant, can determine in an actual way. If this is the case, the metaphysical method should consist in following the direction of a movement already suggested in the affirmation of being. It would no longer be a *conversion* and, so to speak, provisory refusal of being in the effort we are making to comprehend its principle; let's say rather that this decision of thought is a *consent to being*, which we never achieve without a certain penetration, without that common sense which is like an initial orientation towards more metaphysical truths.

Consent to being is first of all the attitude that delivers us from what we will name the seduction of the abstract. Doubtless philosophy is always, in its most receptive, its most generous doctrines, an effort to situate our thought before the concrete, the singular, of existence. But how can we in fact gain access to this? It's not only a matter of considering, in line with the mode of abstract thought, a reality that taken in itself is concrete; it is necessary to focus our consideration expressly on all we are thinking in giving ourselves concrete being as an object. From that point we will be led to pass beyond the determinations. The singular cannot first of all be identified with partial aspects, with perspectives we might take on it; we would effectively be leaving outside our actual consideration the presence of the being, which gives reality to each of the aspects according to which we are grasping it [the singular]. Likewise, the understanding gives us the knowledge of the genera of being in their distinction. However, what permits us to attribute existence to each of them is something other than the fixed object, delimited in thought, since it is present in a variable way in each of these determinations. The concrete being is only such through the reality of a notion that cannot be the object of a consideration similar to each of the others by which we will know, from diverse perspectives, its nature. Determination, then, represents in some fashion the "obstacle" against which our thought comes to stumble, which it must pass beyond when it wants to devote itself to the truth. Let us suppose that, without being clearly aware of these dangers, we keep ourselves solely to this knowledge of the determined. We know that our thought should focus on a reality given in itself, so we will follow the realist instinct and arbitrarily identify the real with the perspectives according to which we are able to consider it. The seduction of the abstract will have led us to realized abstraction. This is the obstacle that the consent to being should help us pass beyond, when we accept to think truly, according to the mode of knowing accessible to us, what we give ourselves by taking being as object, and when we come to think singular existence not according to the understanding's determinations only, but according to the universality of being.

When we have succeeded in regaining concrete being as object, the consent of thought to being will deliver us from the resistance that determination opposes to the progress of our thought. Consent will then become, in the proper sense of the word, the method of metaphysics. Indeed, why is it that the understanding, when taking determination as the appropriate object, fails to resolve by itself the problem of being? Because strictly speaking it doesn't pose it. The abstract is doubtless always incomplete, since it is only such by its reference to the singular, but we are keen to fix at least the partial abstractions, those we can express in scientific results, without going so far as representing to ourselves that incommunicable and doubtless infinite perfection of what is singular. We construct our science of things and our philosophical representation of the real without truly placing ourselves in the presence of this idea that the concrete supposes a presence of another order than that fixed by each of our partial abstractions. Consequently, it's not surprising that we can't be led to the metaphysical principle of the real. It is because we rarely consent to follow the spontaneous movement of thought as it manifests itself, in its starting point, in the objective affirmation. Bound to the determinations that are the sole object of the understanding, we think that being is given to us as one or another of the aspects according to which things present themselves to us. When we say things are, we somehow fix their existence in a given, a characteristic that defines and constitutes them. Doubtless we say that things are, but let's be on guard, the affirmation of existence isn't always a complete victory over the tendency that pushes us first to hold on to determinations, then to realize abstractions. We can indeed give ourselves the representation of an objective world, without realizing exactly all we are saying in affirming it is real, it is extant. Now, with this hypothesis, it is not surprising that thought is unable to go beyond the given in order to grasp its principle. Here, in effect, we have existence considered as a characteristic like the others, although being common to all the things that are, strictly speaking, like a genus. But what is the character of a genus? It is particularly, it seems to us, that the abstraction by which we have defined it renders us incapable of knowing anything more than what we have fixed in that same abstraction. Let us suppose, therefore, that we apply to the idea itself of existence this common schema of our analytic thought. It then becomes determined, fixed in itself, a characteristic that things possess in the same way as many others we can think in an abstract way. And from that point, how would the consideration of being allow us to pass on to that of its principle? Things are, and this is all we have to say about them; we are stopped right from this first affirmation. We do wish to recognize the reality of the world, but the way we represent that existence to ourselves seems somehow to enclose the things within themselves. Thus existence does not entail any beyond, and this is why the analyses of philosophers always appear artificial to us, they always come after the fact, in the representation that doesn't at first imply them. Now this judgment is quite natural if we really have a purely analytic conception of being; how, indeed, would we pass from a partial abstraction or a genus to the ideas that we are leaving aside in this representation?

But it remains to know whether this is really the normal attitude of thought. We say, on the contrary, that it is because we have a purely generic notion of being that we renounce following the movement of metaphysical thought whose natural character we don't recognize anymore. So that our error is not wanting to think, according to all its implications, the idea of being, keeping ourselves to the determinations, allowing thought to slide into realized abstractions, and not being able to ascend to that *unperceived essential* that metaphysics has the task of helping us discern. But let us accept thinking the concrete in terms of being, not of determinations of being; through this consent we will be led to notions and principles that the dialectic links together in an ordered way. The determination of the principle of existence will be included implicitly in the effort by which we will have attempted to think being beyond abstract determinations. This prolonging of the movement of thought beyond the obstacles that it itself creates by fixing itself first in determinations, then in realized abstractions, is in our eyes what could correspond to the idealist conversion, and what, in any case, properly constitutes the intellectual virtue of realism. This is what we are proposing to call the method of consent to being; let us understand by this the consent to the movement of thought that makes the affirmation of being an implicit affirmation of God.

Let us first truly lead our thought to that point where it tries to say to itself all that is included in the affirmation of existence. This effort to conquer diversity, to render it intelligible and to think it, is doubtless not a matter of going, with the means at our disposal, to an intellectual knowledge of the concrete in itself. Besides, such a knowledge does not interest the understanding as such, it doesn't seek to know *quot lapilli jaceant in flumine.*[1] But it is a matter of comprehending what it is to be concrete, how the concrete is possible, and not of grasping what is concrete. The movement of the spirit is thus, in a sense, an abstraction, but it is not the partial abstraction that places us in the presence of genera and species in their distinction, even less so is it realized abstraction; on the contrary, it implies in itself concrete reality, and it is on being itself that it expressly wants to focus its consideration. It is properly the character of philosophy to start from an original reality, as simple as you wish, because it is rich in all the metaphysical elements that entail infinity, singularity, existence; and the amplitude of the consequences should be supported by the apparent simplicity of the starting point. Here is the universe in the variety and intimacy of singular things. Let us not seek to penetrate, through an effort of sympathy and intuition, to the deep knowledge of the real; it is better, rather, in the rigorous effort of a thought entirely unadorned to focus on that alone that offers itself to us and that we ought to justify—the character of singularity as it is tied to the two ideas of existence and infinity, and the character of diversity. The determination of the supreme principle of the real as a whole will be the result of the effort of abstraction, which, thus understood, will have placed us in the presence of being itself and not of one or another of its modalities; the method of metaphysics ought to be this dialectic that, through reflection on the conditions

1. "how many pebbles lie in the river." From Thomas Aquinas, *Summa Theologica*, Q. 94.

of possibility of the judgment of existence, allows us to ascend to the first principle. Let us focus ourselves on this consideration alone, that existence is not a determination like the others. As in the *Meditations*, it is to one idea alone that we should return so as to make fully manifest the consequences it includes in an implicit way: *Manebo obstinate in hac meditatione defixus.*[2]

Consent thus understood will indeed have the value of a method. Because, if the initial affirmation of realism that we mean to maintain is the essential relation of thought to being, their common reciprocity, it is still necessary to recognize that metaphysical thought assumes something that comes from ourselves and carries it further than objectivity on behalf of the determinations of the understanding—this is our consent to being. This will permit us, by joining the universality of being with its first principle, to come back to the original objective affirmation, while according it a value not only of fact, but also of right, in the way that, for example in Descartes, the evidence recognized at first is finally guaranteed by divine veracity. We will be sure that we can affirm concrete being because we cannot affirm it, while trying to think all that is comprehended in our judgment itself, without by this implicitly affirming God. Therefore, the recognition of the first principle will not presuppose the idealist conversion; it [the principle] will really lie in the prolonging of objective thought, on condition that it [thought] knows how to get beyond certain *obstacles* that remove us no less from *truth* than from *value*, that it [thought] achieves a victory over itself, and that it orients itself not towards the closed, but on the side of the open.

Let us follow, then, the movement of the thought that, in order to bring its focus onto concrete being, refuses to grasp existence in the way of other determinations. The judgment of existence is consequently only possible through the idea of the universality of being, present in each of the determinations. It is through the consideration of this original type of unity that thought is going to progress. It would be possible, in one sense, to hold onto pure diversity if one were to consider the real only through the variety of the aspects according to which it offers itself to the understanding; but the movement of thought that leads it beyond determinations allows it to recognize

2. "I shall remain fixed resolutely in this meditation." From René Descartes, *Meditations*, "I: Concerning Those Things Which Can Be Called into Doubt."

that the genera are not incommunicable, and that they are all united in being as the object of the judgment. When thought consents at the same time to its own universality and to that of the object on which it is focusing, it finds itself thereby in the presence of this problem: How to comprehend in terms of being the original diversity of the singulars and yet the reality of their distinctions? It is quite clear that the unity we are going to affirm will not be that of genera and species, because that would leave aside what makes the differences irreducible, since those differences would have to be grasped exteriorly to the genera, while all is common to being, immanent to it. But if this unity we are seeking cannot, in the manner of a genus, be founded on the presence, possibly, of a common element, as humanity is common to all human beings, then it must be founded on the community of a relation. There we recognize the type of unity that we express through the analogical unity and that indicates a proportional similarity: *unum proportione.*[3] Thus, the word vision can be spoken at the same time of a corporeal or intellectual vision, because in both cases there is a relation, intrinsically varied, of the function of knowing to its object. Again, in the same way, divine wisdom and human wisdom retain a certain unity because they entail, one and the other, a reference to being, although in one case the knowledge depends on things, and in the other it is creative. If the analogy thus indicates only the presence of the same relation, it does not risk bringing diversity back to that indistinct community we think in representing to ourselves the unity of genera and species.

Now, nothing prevents us from thinking the unity of being under the aspect of analogical unity, from safeguarding in this way the affirmation of [both] concrete distinction and the unity to which the very idea of existence, distinct from determinations, obliges us to raise ourselves. In order to reach this outcome, it suffices to grasp (somehow inherent in concrete reality) the community, itself always varied, of a relation. It is this community we express by the distinction between essence and existence, by the relationship of one to the other. Consequently, led solely by our concern to think all the metaphysical characteristics of the concrete, to not arrest too quickly the movement of thought, or in a word, to consent to being,

3. "one relationally." From Aquinas, *Summa Theologica*, Q. 92.

we will see ordering themselves the truths that appeared to exclude each other, those of distinction and unity. We affirm the distinction of essence and being in order to render multiplicity possible, since being appears in this way intrinsically varied and doesn't have all the perfection of the simple. But this same relationship, by which we are able to think diversity in terms of being, is in a sense the foundation of unity, since it allows us to think it, not in a generic, but in an analogical way. Finally, as though by a sort of backlash, the analogical unity of being is the guarantee of the very diversity that we recognize on the level of existence, since it does not bear only on those aspects retained in our genera and laws, to which the foundation itself of being would remain extrinsic. These initial consequences are like a victory gained in the attitude of consent. Distinction in unity, in the analogical sense, is affirmed against the habits and perhaps against the requirements of a thought applied to defining and fixing. It is like a victory of metaphysical reason over the processes of the abstract understanding.

The world is one at the same time it is diverse, because the affirmation of its unity is no longer that of a common element into which, in some respect, the solid character of the distinctions would come to be reduced. Therefore, when we situate ourselves in the face of concrete reality, nothing prevents us from maintaining before the metaphysical reflection the characteristics by which it [reality] appears to us in an immediate way, the interior perfection, then the distinction and the unity. Quite to the contrary, it is in terms of being itself that we are thinking these diverse metaphysical aspects of the real; they no longer come to be an obstacle of some sort for each other, but the principle of one is at the same time that of the others. Thought, in prolonging its proper movement, rises spontaneously to the level where metaphysical ideas join each other. But its work is not entirely realized for all that. It is not enough *to think* on the level of metaphysical being; it is still a matter of *explication.* Now we want to show that there is no heterogeneity of one of these functions to the other, as Kant supposes. In order to be raised to the principle of metaphysical explication in which being will be established in its existence, and thanks to which we will succeed in grasping the essential of the metaphysical meaning of the real, it suffices here again not to arbitrarily arrest the movement that, from the thought of being, will lead us to that of its principle. It suffices to consent to all that we are thinking in signifying being, so that the consent, by which thought refuses to determine and arrest itself, becomes, strictly speaking, the very method of metaphysics. It remains for us, therefore, to show how the affirmation of being we are making obliges us, without any consideration extrinsic to this, to affirm the absolute, how we will raise ourselves to recognize its necessity solely by following the movement of thought to which we have only to consent.

Through the consideration of being such as it is given us in the judgment of existence, metaphysical reflection will be led forward in a progression of which we will indicate only the essential principle, and where no artificial step intervenes. Let us not attempt to seek any other starting point towards the absolute than this double consideration of the one and the many in regard to being, an unadorned and strict, but not partial, consideration, as we have doubtless sufficiently shown. This is also, let us note anew here, the most assured method of a metaphysical reflection concerned not to see its results ceaselessly put into question by changes to our representation of the world brought about by the results of the positive sciences. Metaphysics is situated on another plane because its mission is to help us comprehend that itself that makes it so that positive results can be given us, and it is to it that the determination of the principles of the concrete corresponds. Let us not therefore seek to know what is real and diverse; let us fix our thought only on the characteristics thanks to which the world is given to us in its unity, in its distinction. Now, we have been able to establish that distinction only takes its sense from the relationship of essence and being; so it must be that existence, such as we grasp it in our experience, is not that existence that would be given at the same time as the perfection of essence and identified with it. The existence is received from outside and communicated. The beings of our experience don't therefore have their existence through themselves, so that in order to comprehend the very reality according to which they are given to us, we are obliged to suppose another, different nature, able to communicate existence. Only one cannot communicate what one does not possess in oneself, or else under the condition of having received it. Thus we would be looking in vain for the position itself of existence, if we were not to affirm that, beyond the forms according to which it is realized in our experience, it arises in a being where it is not received from outside, but is identified with the perfection itself of its essence. The simple affirmation of multiplicity is therefore a starting point sufficient for the proof of God. We ascend to the absolute if we are entirely faithful to the requirements of our thought, as soon as we affirm that the real presents itself to us under the aspect of diversity. To say, for example, that I affirm the existence of three trees, is to say that no one of them is the totality of being, and that existence is thus limited in its relation with essence; this existence, distinct from essence, is thus received and will find its first principle only in a being that possesses it [existence] by essence.

But the analysis we have sketched has led us also to another result. If the distinction of things is founded on the relationship between essence and existence, the unity we uphold underlying the diversity of concrete things finds its principle in the analogical affirmation, that is in the proportional similarity. Consequently, I can think being as one at the same time I think it as diversified, realized in distinct natures. What, then, is the foundation of this unity that we affirm in an analogical sense? It cannot be found in the specific nature of each thing, since multiplicity cannot by itself account for the unity in which it is gathered. Nor does unity find its foundation in the recognition of a common genus that would encompass all the things that are, because in the sense we are attributing to it, it [unity] would be made to dissolve the real in that abstract, and by itself incomplete, community of genera. Only one conclusion is thus possible, which is that we must seek the foundation of the analogical unity of being in the common relation that all concrete beings maintain to the absolute principle, whose perfection contains eminently and potentially that of all created things. Thus understood, the unity of being is not opposed to the intrinsic diversity of natures, what is more, it is relative to the absolute unity of being by itself.

The proof of God is therefore possible in the two cases only because the idea of relation penetrates that of being, and because when we start with the analysis of concrete being, it [the idea of relation] cannot be detached from it. Through the very characteristics that assure its unity and its distinction, being is relative to God. We don't think being as that which is, in the sense only that it would exclude nothingness, in a consideration that would imply no other; quite to the contrary, the affirmation of concrete being sends thought back to the affirmation of the absolute with which it maintains a necessary relation, so much so that it would be unintelligible without it. The truth is, the argument from causality does not consist here in linking up by an intelligible connection realities at first given; it consists, in a simpler and more metaphysical way, of properly grasping what the characteristics of the real are that we are affirming in its unity and distinction, and in seeing that these characteristics, if we want truly to think them on the level of being and thereby go beyond determination, imply a reference to the absolute of being. In this sense, we can say that consideration of the unity and multiplicity in being is already the consideration of contingency. We haven't had the idea of contingency intervene; inasmuch as it is tied to the consideration of becoming, it would itself moreover, on this level of thinking, have to be thought in connection with being. This is therefore the consideration of being that is essential to metaphysics, its sufficient starting point, all the more inevitable if thought is concerned truly to justify what is given, to move out of partial abstraction with all the conditions this movement entails. Thought will not finally be able to signify being in its representations without implicitly affirming God, because reality, by the very fact that it is recognized on the level of being, in its unity and its distinction, is unintelligible without its relation to God. Thus the act by which I affirm God is not a result that would be somehow foreign to the principle itself of objective affirmation; it only prolongs that movement that already virtually implies it. We won't say that it is God we know in knowing the world, but it is very true to say, in a sense, that the implicit affirmation of God is found in the act of judgment of existence, for those who seek the metaphysical conditions thanks to which it is possible. *Aliquid est, ergo Deus est.*[4]

Thus understood, the determination of the first principle is not a task in which metaphysical thought would be condemned to fail. The relation of the singular to the absolute is, on the contrary, given in the very positing of being when we take it in a metaphysical sense, and to discern its exact nature, it seems to us, is only to pass beyond the point of view that we will call an *isolating philosophy* to that of an *existential philosophy.* Indeed, let us try again to indicate, at the

4. "Something is, therefore God is." From the medieval scholastics, but the exact source is not clear.

end-point of these analyses, the conditions that would render possible the success of the dialectic. Being, we would say, implies relation, and if that is the principle of a realist dialectic, the victory it allows us to win is more difficult than one would think at first. It is due before everything to the effort we must make to consider being otherwise than as the result of a conceptual analysis that would fix it in itself, while isolating it from its principle. Science can always make an abstraction of what exceeds it; moving on the level of experience, it can simply isolate the aspects of the real it is examining from the ensemble of conditions that render them possible. Metaphysics cannot be satisfied anymore with that abstraction; because it seeks the conditions of the ensemble of experience and of existence in general, it really must find them in a principle that is no longer on the level of empirical reality, and that is itself beyond existence as it is distinct from an essence. But how could we come to this vision? We do not easily pass beyond the perspective of generic abstraction because we ordinarily think according to the determinations the understanding offers us. But consequently, believing we are firmly fixing the aspects of the real, we limit and isolate them; we might well say, it is true, that things are, and we know more or less clearly that this isn't exactly to affirm that they have only such or such a determined nature. We soon forget these differences however, and from then on how would we get beyond the simple affirmation of being, how would the judgment of existence furnish us with the impulse to ascend from the level of facts to that of metaphysical necessity? Metaphysical thought will never be born if we represent existence to ourselves according to the type of objectivity that the understanding can determine. If the understanding is incapable of rising beyond the abstractions fixed in its generic concepts, it is by this itself impotent to resolve the problem of being, and if we were solely to follow this direction of thought, we would place ourselves only on the level of phenomenalism and soon even nihilism. But let us try to think according to metaphysical reason, and refuse to give being to ourselves as the communality obtained by the analysis that gives us genera and species. Affirming first that the universe is concrete, let us avoid forgetting so quickly this recognition and doing everything as though in reality it were not so. Situating ourselves on a level beyond that of determination, we will go beyond concrete existence itself up to its proper principle. This is because the representation of concrete being and of existence is grasped as relative to that which surpasses it and what thought can attempt to know. Metaphysical truths therefore are in the prolonging of the affirmation of being that implies them. The judgment of existence, far from arresting thought at the pure representation of the thing, perhaps soon followed by the affirmation of the irrational, gives it [thought], on the contrary, its impetus, and thus allows us to go stage by stage to the recognition of the metaphysical absolute. But, far from making us forget the real, this movement of thought on the contrary draws us back there, and in a certain way we only affirm God metaphysically in order to be more assured of the existence of creatures. Metaphysical explication in effect always presents itself as the victory achieved over a representation of the real that is purely abstract and without depth. Indeed, it is not merely an aspect of the real it allows us to take into account, but what in being is the foundation of its unity and perfection.

This is the movement of thought we would be led to make if we were simply faithful to the method we have called consent to being. If one rules out the vision of a purely irrationalist realism, incapable of truly ensuring the existence that it is content to declare beyond thought, metaphysics can follow only the two methods whose opposition could be expressed as that of conversion or consent. They are analogous in that in both cases being is grasped and explained in a synthetic vision. Idealism seeks, in effect, to identify the reality of concrete beings with the reality of the connection whose nature and truth thought grasps through the reflection it makes on itself. In the metaphysical interpretation we have just followed, the absolute is at the end-point of the judgment [of existence], and it is in the relationship to the absolute that concrete beings possess their proper reality, in their unity and their distinction. If, therefore, we were to consider the judgment as a whole, following its function of absolute reference to the being beyond genera, we would see that it proceeds, in its principle, from a transcendental activity, itself under the divine motion, and that it comes to its end in the transcendent. But the two metaphysical visions, whose analogy we want to indicate, remain quite distinct in their outcome. The consent to being gives to our thought, strictly speaking, an orientation towards *the beyond*. Thus, the nature of the absolute and of the relation it maintains with concrete reality are grasped in a way that is less simple, and in appearance less assured, than they would be following the rhythm of a thought that affirms unity in essence, which realizes the absolute on the level itself of contingency and represents the relationship of metaphysical dependence to itself under the aspect of the necessity that ties thought to its object. But we have tried to show that this philosophical vision would not allow us to get out of pure abstraction, and would soon come to be confused with phenomenalism. One can try to determine the nature of the absolute in some way, but in believing that through the reflection of thought on itself we can possess and determine the higher level of reality, it is actual existence that we miss. The relationship of contingency, as we understand it, implies, it is true, that its superior end-point isn't accessible to us, in the sense that we can't determine it by thought, but it alone goes to the real, to concrete existence. In order to indicate the true significance of the dialectic and the conditions of its necessity, we may therefore be permitted to take up again the expression Lachelier used and say that it is better to affirm the reality of the *beyond* than "the so-called science that, in passing too easily from the idea to being, risks grasping only an ideal being."[5]

5. Lachelier, *Oeuvres*, tome II, *Science et religion*, 165. [Forest's own citation]

4

Being and Relation

We are now in a position to return to the original objective affirmation, about which metaphysical reflection has as its goal establishing in a critical manner the conditions of possibility, the foundations. The course we have followed does not mean that the affirmation of being would be impossible before the affirmation of God, that we couldn't be certain of anything before being certain of the existence of God. Indeed, in that case the uncertainty of the starting point would entail also that of the conclusion we can reach. We simply mean that the affirmation of being doesn't have the same character before and after the dialectic we have followed; we have passed from the order of fact to that of right. Thought can indeed try, without renouncing its own capacity to affirm being, to return on itself and make a judgment about its purpose, its essential orientation, its truth. Likewise, if metaphysical reflection is focused not on thought itself, but on the nature of the being it affirms, it will try to comprehend how being could be joined to its principle, and it is clear that the judgment of existence will, after this discernment, have a new significance in our eyes. However, we are not asking the dialectic only to offer us the possibility of affirming being in right as in fact. The relation that the being that is offered us as object maintains with the first principle should allow us also to know its metaphysical nature, to thereby complete the work itself of reason, beyond the partial abstractions of the understanding, whose proper object is determination. Thus, the affirmation of being will no longer correspond simply to that vision where it is given only on the level of distinctions and genera; it will place us, on the contrary, in a new perspective, because we will be going to the foundation of being in its whole universality. Metaphysical thought indeed supposes a prolonging, a consent that carries it beyond the givens of the understanding; from this it follows that our knowledge of being will be of another nature than that given us by objective thought in its initial form. Therefore, by the fact that, in its complete realizing of itself, thought wants to signify the highest universality, and not merely determination, it allows metaphysics to fulfill its essential function, which is to arrive at making us aware of what existence is.

But metaphysics would lose its rigorous and objective character if the conclusions we are able to reach were not based on the method itself that permits them to be established. Now we have insisted on the analogy that exists between the methods of conversion and consent, because both start from the same awareness of the difficulties to be resolved, because they suppose equally that we pass beyond a certain inadequate form of objective thought. It is thus natural that the conclusions that one reaches correspond to each other in a certain way and one could not, it seems to us, establish the characteristics of a metaphysical vision of being without reflection on the nature and exact bearing of these encounters. It's because these two doctrines will have, the one and the other, that essential characteristic on which all the others perhaps depend, of wanting to finally establish the metaphysical pre-eminence of synthesis over analysis. At the same time as abstraction risks trapping itself, in the vision it offers us of being, in that incomplete, unfinished reality that corresponds to the notions of the understanding, it isolates the elements thus deprived of their very existence even in the separation where they might be maintained. There will therefore only be a philosophy of the concrete through synthesis and, consequently, through a certain metaphysical solidarity of being and relation. But how should this be understood? Idealism is satisfied to substitute for objective being the metaphysical reality of the synthesis in which everything connects and affirms itself as real. But if, as we have tried to show, it is impossible to grasp by this conversion to interiority alone an absolute foundation, a value that is necessary and metaphysical, if the real cannot be identified with the act alone of reference and liaison, it does remain that the metaphysical necessity of the synthesis be somehow implied in the consideration itself of being and that the relative character of the object of our thought be grasped in the nature of the affirmation of existence.

If it is thus, we don't entirely abandon the inspiration of idealism; rather we add to this doctrine the conditions that allow it to be fully realized. From the point of view where we are placed, idealism appears as a provisory philosophy, whose value is to make us anticipate a certain number of truths that metaphysical reason ought to establish in their rigor. In this sense, we can say, in Leibnizian terms, that the doctrine whose orientation we are seeking to indicate *symbolizes with* idealism. They both propose to go beyond an inferior realism, to shed that illusion, more tenacious and difficult to overcome than it seems, from which philosophic thought must keep itself by avoiding confinement to objective determinations, to isolated elements. Thus, in both cases, thought orients itself towards a metaphysical vision, since it only passes beyond objective determinations in order better to ensure the reality from which it starts, and about which the sciences don't succeed in giving us the complete understanding. Let us say, reprising Jules Lagneau's expression, that always "objective experience implies and recovers a metaphysic." We are therefore setting out to comprehend the metaphysical meaning of experience, in a doctrine where the solidarity of being and relation is affirmed in the most definite way.

It is by the same act that metaphysical reflection safeguards the being of concrete things and the aspiration to the universal, uniting in this way the point of view of experience and that of metaphysics. We will say, then, that we raise ourselves beyond the vision of an immediate objectivity when we grasp that the affirmation of being is by itself the recognition of unity and perfection. To place oneself within the metaphysical point of view is first to take the consideration of being and the one to the point where those two notions cease to appear to exclude each other. All our dialectic has in a sense only consisted in seeking a way to avoid the dilemma of Parmenides: "Being is the negation of the one, the one is the negation of being."[1] Now it is quite certain that were we to limit the affirmation of the one to meaning a generic community realized among beings, that unity wouldn't be able to enter into the plane of concrete reality; existence wouldn't be able to participate in it. We think, on the contrary, that there is a way to safeguard unity in diversity, to maintain unity on the level of an existential philosophy; it is to affirm it as a proportional unity. It is even because we have led reflection to this recognition of being that we have been able to discern in concrete existence this type of proportional unity. In this sense, then, we can already say that the objective affirmation has a metaphysical scope, because it leads to grasping being in its unity. Nevertheless, the unity thereby manifested isn't yet captured in all the meaning it comprises. We can doubtless affirm that diversity and unity call to each other in some way; that is, the same metaphysical reflection through which we affirm the universality of being safeguards its intimacy. But this unity is still only that of a communality, a communality doubtless of relation and proportion, not of essence or of generic notion. It is possible to go beyond, that is, to recognize that being is one, in this sense, that the being of our experience constitutes one universe only in which the consideration of synthesis must finally prevail over analysis. That is what should come to be established by a philosophy whose starting point is the recognition of the solidarity of being and relation.

The affirmation of unity understood in this way appears to be the distinctive feature of idealist thought, which, it seems, gives itself the most favorable conditions for bringing it about, because it is the system itself that, in recapitulating the anterior adaptation of the elements, possesses the supreme value and alone acquires effective existence. Yet perhaps the method we have followed would succeed in justifying distinction within unity in a simpler and more immediate way, by giving it definitive value. What is, in effect, the nature of the accord that can be established between the unity through which each thing is itself and the synthesis through which in a sense all things are only one? In the idealist vision, the nature of the relation somehow precedes that of the being and arises as an element of its

1. See Plato, *Parmenides* 141e.

structure before coming progressively to wholly constitute it. In placing ourselves in this perspective, we would find ourselves in the presence of a law not only immanent to things, but more real than the elements it gathers together, because they owe to it their reality. In that way, the nature of the relationship is to a great extent opposed to that of the singular distinction, of the existential diversity. Doubtless, as Hamelin showed, idealism does not set out to dissolve the concrete things into an indistinct unity; it only wants to connect them, to make it so that none is isolated. But we can ask whether it really achieves this end; from the moment being is constituted by relation, it [relation] underlies existences, and constitutes as if a primary reality, fundamental and essential. Thus, the vision of unity corresponds to a more definitive and solid truth than that of distinction. It is not so in the doctrine whose main directions we are following. Relation entails no metaphysical anteriority over existence, in the sense that it [existence] would itself be constituted by it and would appear only as the end result of a series of relations. Quite to the contrary, the reality of relationship is implied in some way in the position itself of the concrete being. Indeed, one cannot affirm the singular reality in a judgment of existence without recognizing that it is contingent, and the contingency entails an essential relation to the absolute; it is contradictory in itself without this relation. It is therefore at the moment we reach existence, and not in the prior order of essences, that the reality of relation appears; thus, it doesn't have to be exceeded in any way. The very character that gives the being its unity and the intimacy that distinctively constitutes it, leads to what is beyond, and it is in this sense, in a definitive way, that its being is to be relative. Consequently, we cannot, it is true, grasp the nature of the synthesis under the form of that connection that is woven into the plane of the elements themselves, which is entirely immanent to them and enters into the constitution of their essence. But the solidarity of being and relation leads us to recognize the synthesis through a principle superior to the elements it is assembling, and it is the nature of that connection that permits us to establish in a simpler, more solid way the relations of God and the world. Indeed, from the moment when each being grasped on the level of experience is such only through the absolute of being, it is this reality superior to the level of experience that can unify the real. One shouldn't fear that from this viewpoint connection is assured in a less complete way than in the philosophy of pure immanence. Doubtless we are no longer in the presence of a unity in essence, but the nature of the *vinculum*[2] necessary to the organization of the universe isn't less solid outside the plane where the things are themselves assembled. It possesses, we know, all the solidity of the relation that penetrates to the intimacy of the concrete; it has no accidental and superficial character. But, inversely, the synthesis no longer risks diminishing the consistency, the interior perfection of each being, because the principle that permits it to be established assumes on the contrary that already-constituted existence. Thus, the law of the formation of the whole is not immanent to the parts; thought raising itself beyond the level of concrete existences grasps their harmony at the same time as their internal unity, and perceives the original connection that makes it so that those two notions, far from being opposed, on the contrary call to each other and determine each other reciprocally.

The synthetic connection thus unites the diversity of beings in one and the same universe. Let us add that it penetrates into distinction in an absolutely immediate way, and we will see willingly in this notion of the *immediate* what corresponds in a certain manner to the idea of *immanence*, because it allows for the recognition of a certain presence of the absolute in the singular. We will never affirm the being of an element that we would begin by cutting off, by isolating from the totality. This is to say that the reality of the singular appears to us when we see it as one of the possible aspects, one of the forms of realization of being in general. Such is the vision that gives its metaphysical sense to the affirmation of being and renders it possible. But what is now that universal nature we should affirm, and how could it play the role of a principle? We know well enough, because we have shown in many ways, that being will not be that generic communality[3] that thought at first affirms when it raises itself still feebly above

2. The Latin term used by Forest was adopted directly into English vocabulary, and while commonly used in anatomy as another name for "ligament," also has the rarer meaning, closer to Forest's sense, of "unifying bond."

3. The French *communauté* used by Forest here and in several places hereafter can also be translated as "community." I have chosen the rarer English term "communality," the condition or state of relating to a community, because it seems to me less potentially misleading in conveying Forest's meaning.

the empirical givens. Thus understood, the unity of being wouldn't be of any help to us in our effort to discern metaphysical principles. Starting from the recognition of an element by itself isolated, incapable of supporting the weight of an affirmation of existence, we would be led to another element, also entirely incomplete, isolated and abstract. The unity of being is therefore of another nature. It's not at all that of a genus, still less that of a substance that would be some sort of screen between the singular and the absolute. By the very manner in which we consider the proportional unity of being, we are led to think that it finds its foundation only in the diverse participation of each being in the unity of being by itself. Concrete existence returns, then, to the idea of being in general of which it is only a realization, and the unity of being thus understood, far from arresting thought at an abstract nature, makes it possible to affirm the perfection of absolute existence.

Thus, when thought raises itself from the singular to the universal, it doesn't risk being fixed in the consideration of the abstract; it ascends to the absolute, which reaches directly into the intimacy of concrete things. It doesn't have to reflect, like synthetic idealism, on the conditions of the passage from the abstract to the concrete, it doesn't have to seek to make thought real by allowing it to go beyond the sphere of abstraction and emptiness, because it never situates itself on that level of incomplete elements. When the dialectic, raising itself from the concrete to the absolute, brings about the "passage from one genus to another," how would it cease to hold itself in the presence of being, according to the diverse modalities where it [being] can be realized? Nothing comes to insert itself, so to speak, between being and being, because there is no metaphysical intermediary between the divine simplicity and the intrinsic unity of the concrete being. Therefore, metaphysical thought, which has the property of putting aside all physical distinction of the being whose interior plenitude it affirms, seeks the conditions that allow it to use analysis, understood in a metaphysical sense, for recognition of the actual reality of immediate givens. Indeed, just as, following Aristotle's demonstration, the abstract cannot be substance, so we will add that at no moment could it be principle. The absolute to which the dialectic leads us is grasped in its actual perfection, much simpler and richer than that of the Hegelian *concrete universal.* Thought raises itself from being to being without the ideal genesis of the real following in any way the progression of abstract notions, like that abstract possibility of thought to which the principles of idealism bring us, but that can't in any way play the role of metaphysical principle of being itself.

Metaphysical reflection therefore provides in a definitive way its foundation to a philosophy of unity and of synthesis, a doctrine where unity penetrates in an immediate manner into the plane of singular diversity, even though its principle is superior to the assembled elements. Thus, the metaphysical affirmation, under the form where we are actually considering it, that of unity, really focuses on the being itself of experience. In a sense, it is possible to affirm, not that there is only one being, but that being is one, a unity of proportion and synthesis. The affirmation of unity would perhaps seem to be more metaphysical than that of diversity, because the latter is more apparent, more manifest. Nevertheless, they cannot be opposed, but imply one another; consequently, the recognition itself of diversity takes on a metaphysical value that it didn't have in immediate experience. It acquires, indeed, a more solid and definitive significance when we are assured that it won't be threatened by the consideration of the one towards which metaphysical thought raises itself spontaneously.

It remains for us to consider a consequence of another order that we should bring to light in trying to grasp the true meaning taken on by the very fact of being real. The accord we have sought to show between distinction and unity becomes also that which establishes itself between being and perfection, or, for quite analogous reasons, between the real and ideal. The philosophy of analogy does not, indeed, lead only to a doctrine of order and synthesis. The synthesis, we were saying, is not founded only on the relation, implied in the essence itself, of each concrete being to the absolute of being. It is therefore not a matter of affirming only a principle of unity, which orders things from the outside and without penetrating them; rather, it is a matter of first recognizing in the nature of each contingent being a relation to the absolute of being, and founding upon the communality of this relation the order in which they are all assembled. Consequently, the absolute is not like another order of being out of all proportion to that of experience; in the act itself by which we raise it above the relative, we grasp it as the highest perfection, of which the concrete being in its very nature is an incomplete realization. In raising ourselves towards the absolute of being, the consideration of the concrete helps us to grasp a perfection realized within limits that existence itself disregards when we take it in the perfection of its idea. If, therefore, we strip away from the notion of tendency all reference to our subjective experience, we will be able to say that every concrete being, in the truth of its metaphysical nature, is a tendency toward perfection.

This is the same movement of thought that can help us grasp the originality of the connection that establishes itself between the real and the ideal. One of the most habitual attitudes of philosophic thought, that which, as we know, idealism in particular adopts, consists in seeking somehow on this side of existence itself the ideal nature, what would be the true nature of things, what they possess in thought and which sensible reality manifests only on the outside. This is because when we seek to determine the principles capable of supporting the very reality of our experience, we can at first turn away in a provisory manner from the existence it is a matter of reaching. It is with this methodical refusal, not with consent, that we might get to being. Reality would thus be grasped in its essence, or its idea, as it is, not in itself, but in thought. The dialectic consists, then, in showing that, far from missing actual existence in this way, we are on the contrary ensuring it more solidly and definitively, because, in the connection it constitutes, thought gives to phenomena the being they don't have by themselves. So one comprehends how being appears in a manner fully ideal, intelligible, since it is through the action of the spirit that nature develops. It seems, on the contrary, that in going toward the recognition of the incommunicable being of the singular, one thereby renders oneself incapable of recognizing within it this ideal character, because the substantial depth of being, posed at first, is doubtless what evades the idea, what can't be determined as essence. However, the method we have followed permits us to think nothing of the kind, and is perhaps going to allow us to establish the accord of being and ideal in a more solid way. Let us note first that the presence of the universal, understood in the sense of the idealist syntheses, in the singular reality risks remaining abstract because it is anterior to the position of being, and because it isn't certain that we can reach actual existence by a progression through the abstract. But following the method we have adopted, the ideal nature that the real manifests isn't anterior to it in the sense that it would be like an element enabling us to end up at its concrete structure. On the contrary, it is at the moment when we grasp existence in what it has of the incommunicable, in its very intimacy, that we raise ourselves to recognize the universal nature of being, and then the principle of this communality in absolute being. Such is, finally, this universal nature that the singular can express through its being. Now, the universal is still the ideal, if the idea is opposed to the real as that which is not given, that which can't be grasped and posed in a purely empirical way. It is thus really existence itself, not some of its anterior determinations, that presents an ideal value and can only be like a manifestation of the universal. Just as being isn't opposed to the one, so it doesn't form a screen to the intelligible, it isn't that depth of irrational reality that the idea wouldn't be able to reach. The absolute reality of the ideal, that is to say, this truly concrete universal present through analogical participation in the very position of the particular, isn't on this side of concrete existence nor even uniquely beyond it, in the sense that it [concrete existence] would be altogether foreign to it. The absolute doubtless exceeds the relative in every way, but it is right to its substantial depth that reality is a manifestation of ideal existence raised beyond experience and nature, that is, [a manifestation] of God himself. In order to grasp the nature of the ideal, it is useless to reduce the concrete to a pure essence existing only in thought. It is enough to affirm it on the level itself of concrete reality, because the opposition of the real and ideal disappears for a metaphysical vision of being. It's in this vision, at least glimpsed, that things take on the meaning that the poets and philosophers try to translate in diverse ways, and that constitutes what we call their truth, that is their real being in its relation to the ideal.

The analogy we have just noted would perhaps allow us to say that the doctrine to which we are led can be called indifferently realism or idealism. It is the essence of idealism to affirm that thought can only grasp the reality that would be adequate to it or superior to it: νοῦς ὑπὸ τῶν νοητῶν κινεῖται.[4] But in the act by which thought grasps the real, it is led further; beyond the fact, it is really the idea that is the object of thought, as it expresses and manifests itself in the

4. "thought is moved by what is thinkable." This seems to be a paraphrase of Aristotle's *Metaphysics* 1072.

perfection of the concrete being. The interpretation we are proposing could therefore, in a sense, be presented as an *idealism of the concrete.* Or rather, let us say in simpler fashion, and in order in every way to avoid any misunderstanding that could arise, that it is a *metaphysical vision of the concrete*, in which the immediate relation of the singular to the absolute prohibits us from holding ourselves to the consideration of the facts by themselves and allows us, on the contrary, to regain in the fact the reality of the idea. The concrete possesses in its being the perfection of the intelligible that it manifests. It is therefore, in this sense, the idea that is the object of our thought, at least in an indirect way; intellectual illumination remains the final condition of knowledge, whether the spirit be united directly with God or enlightened by the realities in which the truth of the intelligible expresses itself for us. A metaphysic of the concrete doesn't therefore risk forgetting, in accord with what M. Lavelle advises, that "the ideas are mediators between God and us," but it is the very reality of the concrete that has itself become ideal, because it is nothing apart from the relation through which it expresses, in its very being, the universal in its absolute nature, the ideal raised above nature. Metaphysics thereby helps us to regain the intelligible in the real, and according to Leibniz's expression, so much in keeping with our analyses, in "that immense subtlety of things that always envelops an actual infinity." The truth of metaphysics, therefore, really is finally the *vision in God*, if we take care not to affirm it only for intelligible nature, which would leave to the side being itself, and if the movement of thought really starts from the facts known to us and not merely the ideas that represent them. This is because reality and the idea cannot be opposed, and the more being appears fixed in itself, incommunicable and rich in its singularity, the more we are invited to go beyond what it is in itself. There is thus a kind of "reversal from for to against," or to employ Hegelian language, after that of Pascal, we will speak of the process of *Aufhebung*, by which what is gone beyond is not repudiated, but found again on another level.

The originality of the doctrine of analogy is therefore that it leads us beyond the objective vision and the inferior realism, but through the consideration of being itself. The objective affirmation, if it is led up to the level of being as such, will cease to appear to us "like the bottom of an impasse." It is thus not exactly a matter of reprising the conclusions of idealism, but of following this movement of thought while making use of it, of entering, as synthetic idealism invites us, into the metaphysical truth of existence. One will be able to pass beyond idealism only in order better to justify the conclusions that its method of conversion to interiority doesn't entirely suffice to establish. If, indeed, the metaphysical truth of existence is the affirmation of unity, of perfection, and of the ideal, we think we have connected them to the nature of being in a more solid way than classical idealism could. Indeed it [classical idealism] remains interlinked with a philosophy of distinction, and that's why the victory of unity and of perfection finally appears to us incomplete, the vision proposed to us remains abstract. The idealist method condemns this doctrine, contrary to its original aim, to a separation of the real from the intelligible, essence from being. It would doubtless like to affirm unity and the idea, but it turns away at the first from consideration of the fact, gives itself the reality of the intelligible at first posed, independently of the existence that will finally be difficult for it to reach, and produces at the first, under the form of relation, a unity incapable of penetrating right to singular diversity. We think, on the contrary, that philosophy ought to go in some sense in the direction of greatest resistance, not to begin by assuming at the first the realization of what it must establish, and starting out from the level of diversity and experience, to recognize in what sense their truth includes a metaphysical affirmation. It is in this sense that the doctrine of analogy symbolizes with idealism, and that this incomplete philosophy helps us only to glimpse truths that its method doesn't entirely justify. We are thus only going beyond synthetic idealism in order better to establish the metaphysical truth of experience.

A metaphysical vision always refuses to bring the substantial depth of being back to the givens alone that experience allows us to grasp, whether to objective experience with the inferior realism, or even to internal experience with idealism. It doesn't consist in somehow enlivening the thought of being by elements borrowed from our psychological experience; it is, rather, a matter of regaining, with a view to passing beyond abstraction, the intimate union of being and relation. But this solidarity is exactly what a philosophy of analogy comes to express. With this notion of analogy, we have, it seems to us, the idea that gives its full sense to the metaphysical affirmation of concrete being. If it is true that we must renounce grasping the reality of the absolute, whether as a given or as an internal act, we are raised by the analogical affirmation to the recognition of the universal, of perfection. Everything is thus metaphysical because everything is analogical, from the moment where thought tries to place itself beyond all abstract determination. This is the truth that, it seems to us, philosophy has as its mission to recall unceasingly; our experience in its highest form sometimes suffices to help us sense the truth that the depth of being is never a simple system of objective givens, determined by the understanding, that it entails a reference to the beyond, and that being is not realized exclusively according to the form grasped by our experience itself. However, human reflection can't be satisfied with this still imperfect and incommunicable intuition. It wants to justify what intuition is able to sense and, connecting the idea of relation to that of being, recognizing in the real an absolute reference, it carries the idealist inspiration as far as the rigor of an existential philosophy. It thus joins in a definitive way the point of view of experience to that of metaphysics. Idealism undertakes to make us see all things within an absolute immanent to reason, and if it can't get there exactly, nothing prevents us from giving to experience the fullness of its metaphysical meaning in a doctrine that raises itself to the absolute, instead of supposing it known prior to the relative.

5

The Spiritual Possession of Being

Metaphysical explication doesn't exactly find its proper end in itself. It constitutes the ensemble of steps by which thought raises itself to contemplation as to a beyond and a complement of another order. But if it is true that the nature of a movement is known by the final end to which it is relative, it is contemplation that should help us comprehend the *raison d'être* of the progress of thought in its effort of explication. Now it has appeared to us that the amplitude of thought was in rapport with the universality of the metaphysical being on which it focuses. Thus, the correspondence between nature and thought is established in a doctrine that sees in knowledge an effort by which it seeks in some way to possess being, and not only to grasp itself in its act. Indeed a philosophy of relation couldn't be satisfied with establishing, on the foundation of analogy, the ordered diversity of the real; it must yet make understood the original nature of the relation that is established between being and knowledge. Consequently, if contemplation appears, in this pause by which the spirit returns to the very science it has acquired, as a spiritual possession, this original idea must also give its meaning to the explication itself. This [explication] participates in the possession by rendering it possible, while contemplation realizes it. Now we would like to show that under these two forms, one preliminary and the other definitive, the possession of being by the spirit, which is properly what we call truth, supposes a very particular attitude of thought, and even in a sense of will. It is this attitude we have called consent, and in returning to some of our preceding analyses in order better to show their significance, we will try to show how the doctrine of analogy conceives not only the essential dependence of thought on being, but also, from the perspective of the subject himself, the nature of this orientation and of his personal attitude before the being offered to him as object.

First, how could one say that explication is possible only through consent? It is manifest enough that it [explication] assumes from its initial movement a concern, already by itself original, to go beyond what the positive sciences permit us to attain. How could we comprehend even the posing of the metaphysical problem if a certain attitude of spirit before the object wasn't adopted from its first steps? We wouldn't get there if we were simply to propose extending step by step, while maintaining their specific nature, the reflections of positive science. Between science and metaphysics is found all the difference between a reflection worthwhile for an aspect of the real and one that goes beyond all determinations. It is thus necessary in order to situate oneself on the level of metaphysical knowledge to make the passage from the particular to the universal in some sort of immediate way, and to render oneself capable of returning from one to the other. But we can add, in more precise fashion, that this attitude peculiar to thought, with which explication begins and progresses, is a consent. Indeed, metaphysical explication supposes the rigorous determination of a problem such that the most far-reaching conclusions can be drawn from its solution alone, and the search for a method that is by itself capable of leading us there. The problem is that of the metaphysical meaning of the concrete, the method is that of consent to being. The peculiarity of partial abstractions, we are saying, is that they are arrested, fragmented, and one will never be able to draw from them any knowledge bearing beyond what is fixed in this abstraction itself. But thought will be able to discern the principles of a metaphysics of relationship and progression by this alone, that it places itself before being, because the notion of being, like that of unity, which is convertible to it, is precisely what we can never identify with a series of abstract determinations. Just by posing it like this, it [the notion of being] leads, contrary to the determinations of the understanding, beyond what we believe we have grasped expressly in our affirmation. Consent to being is thus the method peculiar to metaphysics because it entails the refusal of partial abstraction.

We understand by consent a certain victory of thought, but it is a victory over itself, over its own hesitations, over the possible arrest of its impulse. What is demanded of us is first really to accept treating the object that is offered to us as being. But the tenacious illusion of thought is that we believe we grasp as being what we nonetheless don't stop wanting to limit, to determine, believing we better ensure its possession by fixing it, though on the contrary we thereby threaten it. In our daily experience, or again in science, we treat being hardly as more than one or other of the particular aspects that nevertheless are possible only through its universality. Metaphysics is first of all an effort to overcome this isolation and this hesitation to think being in the beings. In the second place, consent bears on the movement that makes us pass from the affirmation of beings to that of the absolute. Thought would not feel itself threatened in its possession of the real by the metaphysical affirmation that, on the contrary, alone gives it solidity. But it must not arrest its proper progress, [must not] hesitate to prolong the movement that carries it along. It would be enough, then, truly to place oneself in the perspective appropriate to metaphysical thought in order to grasp thereby the method that allows, following a natural order, the resolution of the problem that is being posed. Thus, the difficulties in metaphysical investigation arise only from us, not from the nature of the real offered to us, and that would by itself be unintelligible or antinomial. Just as in Bergson's doctrine intuition takes its value from this alone, that it avoids the deformations of the abstract understanding and somehow lifts the veils the intelligence interposes between the real and us, so the doctrine of consent to being describes the experience that allows everyone to regain, along with the true positing of the metaphysical problem, the method that suffices to resolve it when they renounce a refusal that can only come from themselves. Consent is, so to speak, a kind of victory at the same time that it is an attitude of fidelity; it carries us further than the objective thought of an immediate realism; it is a progressive movement that, beyond hesitation or retreats, establishes us in the truth of our spiritual nature and in the truth of being. Consent is the attitude of spirit that is focused on what there is of the more metaphysical in the thought of being.

Let us add that the attitude of consent, which has rendered explication possible, defines the nature of the contemplation it allows. That contemplation bears at the same time on the specific truth of singular existence and on the ordered diversity of being, that is to say on its unity. Now, we can say that through consent this very reality is made manifest to us in a more complete way. We know that the object of our thought truly possesses for itself that type of existence that we already recognized in it spontaneously; for our critical reflection, being doesn't correspond only to an appearance, a subjective illusion, perhaps relative to our way of thinking. Metaphysical reflection destroys this kind of hesitation, this reserve that we sometimes feel in the face of being, and to which the tradition of the idealist doctrines bears witness in so evident a way. We know that being will not throw up an obstacle to the demands of our thought, and that far from being the dupes of an illusion, we will, on the contrary, be responsive to all its demands in giving ourselves being as object. The natural movement of our thought has rendered useless that conversion, that return of thought onto itself through which it perhaps seemed we were obliged to pass in order to get to the principle of singular existence. Having completed the dialectical effort of thought, we know that we can consent truly to the thought of being, in such a way that the perfection and solidity of our contemplation, or better, of our possession, are somehow the recompense for the attitude we have taken. But this knowledge doesn't settle only on the act of affirming the real; it is like a movement ceaselessly repeated in order to grasp the diversities and discern the correspondences within it. At this moment, the course of thought is still, strictly speaking, only a consent to being; we mean that thought, faithful to its proper nature, by giving itself being as object avoids the illusions that would arise naturally along its route if it adopted another attitude. One of the most tenacious of the illusions of thought is certainly the pretention of wanting to know only by the method of reduction and analysis. To explicate is not to consider in an artificial way one aspect of the real in order to reduce all the others to it, but always to seek the inner communion of diversity in the one. This being the case, if thought lets itself proceed under the weight of that seduction coming from itself, and from that sort of primal gravity that attaches us to determinations, it would soon be no more than abstract reason. By this alone, that it gives itself being as object, truly consenting to all this orientation implies, it will render itself capable of realizing the work of concrete reason, that is, of reason that, taken in the perfection of its idea, seeks to realize among all beings the harmony of their proportions and their relations. We can say, in this sense, that we don't give ourselves being as object of contemplation without consenting to the reciprocity and the relationships implied in the position itself of each singular reality. The types of our experience are diverse, situated at unequal degrees of perfection. We would destroy the reality we want to affirm in them if we were not to grasp those relations. To think being in the truth of its nature is thus to consent to that diversity, to realize the passage not from same to same, but from unity to plurality, as also from one genus to another. For that we have only to let ourselves be led by the nature itself of the object we are considering, refusing only to arrest our contemplation, or refusing to seize in one aspect of the real the image and expectation of a higher perfection. Consent thus understood is only a form of respect, in which we must see the proper virtue of intellectual knowledge; to think is, before all else, to respect the essences. Let us note that in this way we don't affirm the diversity of perfection any less than that of existence; thus, the demands of morality are themselves founded on the objective affirmation as much as on the character of our will. Metaphysical contemplation, then, grows out of the respect and fidelity of thought to the unitary diversity of experience. In a word, the proper object of consent is order.

But to succeed in understanding the originality of this attitude, we would like to reflect on the analogy we can recognize in it with that which idealism proposes we adopt. We have perhaps shown sufficiently that in the idealist philosophy the spirit is as if inclined towards the spiritual possession of being. But according to those doctrines, this possession couldn't be assured for us through contemplation only; thought wouldn't be able to remain as if before a tableau that it would only have to contemplate, and the principle of being does not remain foreign to the act itself of our thinking. Idealism, we know, leads us to see the unity of being in an absolute immanent to reason. It never establishes concrete beings in an independent existence, but wants to place itself at the point where it grasps them as eternally deducted from the reality of the absolute. Idealism thus places itself neither exclusively in the plane of contingent existence, nor exclusively in that of the absolute, but so to speak, between one and the other. Now, this act that constitutes the connection and, more profoundly, even the substantial heart of being, is that in which our reason participates when it raises itself to the level of truth. Therefore, the presence of being corresponds to an act that is realized in us and that we can make ours. This presence is no longer known only from the outside, it is not met with exclusively in an experience; instead, it is effectuated, and we can say literally that in affirming truth we enter into the creative act. We are no longer foreign and indifferent to being, since it has no other substantial heart than this absolute movement, which realizes itself in the reasonings of true thought. One can therefore say that idealism is always a voluntarism, and that it anticipates at the same time the spiritual possession of being and so to say access to the absolute, not from objective contemplation, but rather from our interior act.

The doctrine of consent results in the conclusion that we possess being in a contemplation where the essential dependence of thought in relation to being is manifested. But, in the first place, intellectualism doesn't claim to ignore the truth that voluntarism might include; it's not a matter of allowing no place for the will in the movement that carries us towards being, but only of showing that the object itself of intellectual knowledge isn't the pure result of our autonomous act. We haven't ceased showing that to the nature of objective thought corresponds an attitude proper to the subject himself. But no intellectualism could say that this recognition casts a shadow over the truths it is its mission to defend. What is our concern, in effect? To show the necessity for thought of renouncing the habits that come from imperfect intellection and that, far from being contained in the truth of its nature, on the contrary, arrest it and weigh it down. Consent thus understood is without doubt a matter of will, but immanent to the movement of thought and intended to ensure its perfection. What is more, it is the thought of being that determines the nature of the attitude we should take towards it, that obliges thought to make itself sufficiently welcoming and sufficiently universal to correspond to it fully. Thus, it's not a matter of returning either to a pure voluntarism, according to which the object known is the product of an act, or to a moral dogmatism that seeks to enliven the thought of being, by itself insufficient, through what the movement of the will and the heart help us grasp. It still remains that we have to want to place ourselves within the perspective where alone we can see, within the orientation that will allow us to move forward. We will thereby have nothing to add to the thought of being in order to grasp it in its metaphysical nature; that's not to say that nothing is demanded of us and that the working of metaphysical thought is carried out in some sort of mechanical way. We in fact have to consent, that is, to refuse to limit or even destroy what we are thinking, and by this very act we will regain it in the truth of its being. In this way, the demands of objective thought and the truth of moral dogmatism come into agreement. We have nothing to add to the thought of objective being that would come from ourselves, except consent to the very thing we might neglect, its character of totality, of unity. Consent is thus really the very method of metaphysics, not in the sense of applying a rigid formula, but in the sense of the method entailing an orientation of thought by which it will be given it to move forward. We will progress to the actual conquest, realized over partial abstraction, of metaphysical being on the condition that we add to this thought that alone that comes from ourselves, and that we could possibly refuse, our consent of thought to being. It must perhaps be added finally that, beyond metaphysical knowledge, all the highest forms of the spiritual life assume this constant attitude that is of the nature of consent.

This movement of thought and will perhaps finally places us closer to the absolute than it would have first seemed. One will have noticed that idealism itself employs the term of consent in the most solid of its doctrines, particularly that of Jules Lagneau. But there it's about the consent of thought to itself, to its own ideal nature, and not to being. Now, if it is doubtful that the attitude of thought understood in this way is enough by itself to help us enter into the truth of the absolute, the consent to being, far from pushing us away from it, brings about in us, on the contrary, a kind of participation in the absolute. We mean by that, at the moment, the act from which real being and possible being eternally proceed. Let us note first that objective thought, situated on the level of metaphysical reflection, suffices by itself to help us grasp in being the dependence on this act. Being, we were saying, doesn't appear to us only as a fixed system of essences, a system of givens. It never realizes itself in a cosmos that would have its subsistence in itself, independently of the absolute, and would thus threaten the impulse of the spiritual life. From concrete being we rise to the absolute, without nonetheless being able to find a connection of pure necessity from one to the other. Logic never reaches into the sphere of absolute existence. If indeed we see the necessity of rising from the contingent to the necessary, because it's the only way of not rendering its very existence contradictory, nothing permits us, on the contrary, to lay down any logical necessity in the passage from necessary existence to dependant being. It is, in fact, the meaning of this relation we want to express in speaking of the world's contingency. Consequently, the truth of concrete being isn't grasped independently of its relation to a will, because the absolute is a free act and not only a logical existence. Therefore, one could already say that onto an intellectualist philosophy from the human perspective must be superimposed a voluntarist philosophy from God's perspective.

Guided by these remarks, we can now comprehend how the act of spiritual possession of being helps us enter in some way into the reality of the absolute. In effect, by consenting to being, thought doesn't stop at objective existence; the truth of this existence is finally what the divine will determines with respect to it. That being the case, by the very fact that we are thinking the truth of being in a metaphysical way, it is that will we are somehow making ours. Doubtless the point of application of our will is not in an immediate way the eternal act from which being proceeds; we don't have to make it so that being is and thus bear the weight of the world's existence through thought. Our thought bears on being, but precisely in accepting to give itself being for object and to think it in all its metaphysical implications, it is the very will of God that it reproduces in itself, according to its condition as creature. Consent from our point of view corresponds to creation from the point of view of God; being is only the intermediary, which, far from making a screen between ourselves and the absolute, allows us to give our act a significance itself absolute.

Thus, the doctrine of analogy doesn't only establish in an objective vision the proportional unity of the being given to us and of God; it recognizes also the analogical unity of the act by which we carry ourselves towards being, in seeking to possess it, and the act by which God creates it. Indeed, if intellectual knowledge proceeds from a will, under the form of consent, it doesn't finally focus on an object fixed in itself, but rather on a truth that is such only in its relation to a willing. But it is impossible not to recognize a certain unity in these two forms of will, because they have the same object. When thought makes itself more and more welcoming of being, consenting to see it in its metaphysical truth, consenting thereby to use itself well in this knowledge, the object towards which it is carried, that is being, is exactly that which is the object of the divine will. Consent thus reproduces the divine will in us in an analogical and participatory fashion through the intermediary of being. Now, this unity assumes the presence in what is by participation of what is by itself. Thus, to the proof that grasps the existence of God as cause of the object of our thought is added the proof that grasps it as the cause itself of our spiritual act and present in us in this act. We are considering it here as the act of consent, that is, of the will inherent in some way in the intelligence, relative to contemplation, as one could also, in another way, consider in itself the nature of intellectual knowledge, in order to establish the same type of proportional unity of God with us. In fact, if consent renders being present for us, as creation constitutes it in its truth, there is from one to the other a certain spiritual communality, and we can say, in this sense, that an absolute and metaphysical significance is manifested in the will underlying our intellectual knowledge. Consent is the spiritual attitude that realizes in the highest way within the philosophic order, though not in an exclusive way, our participation in the absolute.

The analyses that are now completed therefore lead us to the same conclusion that the course of our thought allows us to present in two convergent ways. It appears to us, first, that thought raises itself to the absolute only in passing through being. The judgment that focuses on the existence of the diverse is by that very act the recognition of the universal, and from another point of view, we don't grasp in intellectual knowledge our dependence without this recognition being at the same time recognition of the absolute and of our union with it. Thus, the essential metaphysical idea is not that of the act that, according to idealism, would constitute with and through us the reality of being at the same time as that of the absolute; it is, instead, the idea of orientation and reference. Indeed, it is through this idea that philosophy fulfills its whole task, and without drawing on resources other than those proper to it, raises itself at least to the naming of the first love. But inversely, we recognize that we don't have to fear we will push too far the demand for universality and the absolute which animates metaphysics. Indeed, we don't know how far our representation of the real might slide into emptiness and disorder, if it weren't supported by the metaphysical affirmation. This [affirmation] doesn't destroy the specific reality of the contingent and relative; it anchors it, on the contrary, in a doctrine where everything is one, but through the unity of correspondences and relations, where thought achieves the spiritual possession of being through a contemplation that is a created participation in the creative act. Just as we don't have to fear refusing ourselves to God in opening ourselves to creatures, so consent to being isn't the spontaneous movement and as if abandonment, which would have us yield to the solicitation of things; it is the metaphysical method that allows us to see them in their relation to their principle, and in this discernment gives to our attachment to being its spiritual meaning.

Select Bibliography

(Works Cited in the Foreword and Introduction)

Saint Augustine. *Confessions.* Translated by Henry Chadwick. Oxford: Oxford University Press, 1998.

Dante Alighieri. *La Vita Nuova.* Translated by Barbara Reynolds. Harmondworth, UK: Penguin, 1969.

Forest, Aimé. *Du consentement à l'être et autres textes.* Edited by Philippe-Marie Margelidon. Paris: Hermann, 2022.

———. "Itinéraire philosophique." *Vichiana* 3 (1965) 54–74.

———. "La recherche philosophique." Appendix to *Du consentement à l'être et autres textes,* edited by Philippe-Marie Margelidon, 87–114. Paris: Hermann, 2022.

———. *Nos promesses encloses.* Paris: Beauchesne, 1985.

Heidegger, Martin. *What Is Called Thinking?* Translated by J. Glenn Gray. New York: Harper & Row, 1972.

Oakeshott, Michael. *Experience and Its Modes.* Cambridge: Cambridge University Press, 2015.

Plato. *Parmenides.* In *The Collected Dialogues of Plato,* edited by Edith Hamilton and Huntington Cairns. Princeton: Princeton University Press, 1961.

www.ingramcontent.com/pod-product-compliance
Lightning Source LLC
LaVergne TN
LVHW090531110826
845146LV00003B/1056

* 9 7 9 8 3 8 5 2 3 9 7 2 6 *